I LOVE MONEY

"WHEN YOU PAY ATTENTION TO MONEY IT STARTS GROWING"

2ND EDITION

SURESH PADMANABHAN

JAICO PUBLISHING HOUSE

Ahmedabad Bangalore Bhopal Bhubaneswar Chennai
Delhi Hyderabad Kolkata Lucknow Mumbai

Published by Jaico Publishing House
A-2 Jash Chambers, 7-A Sir Phirozshah Mehta Road
Fort, Mumbai - 400 001
jaicopub@jaicobooks.com
www.jaicobooks.com

I LOVE MONEY
ISBN 978-81-7992-871-4

First Jaico Impression: 2008
Seventh Jaico Impression (Revised Edition): 2011
Eighth Jaico Impression: 2012

Printed by
Anubha Printers
Plot No. 19, Udyog Kendra Extn.1
Ecotech-III, Greater Noida U.P. 201308

Dedication

Dedicated to all those who love Money, to those who would love Money after reading this book and to India my Motherland one of the greatest nations of the world.

Please paste a symbolic representation of Money.

I Love Money!

Let every cell of your being reverberate with feelings of Money Love. This pure state of Love will throw open the floodgates of Money flow in your life.

Please paste a picture of yourself. (I hope you are smiling in it.)

I love and accept myself as I am.

You are looking at the most Powerful Person in the World: YOURSELF.

All the Money that you've ever made or will make, will originate from your Personal Powers. Connect deep within and manifest your Ultimate Potential.

Please paste a symbolic representation of the
Superior Power – God/Existence/Universe.

*I trust the Power greater than me to
manifest my ultimate potential.*

Think of the existing abundance and vastness of our
Universe/God/Existence and let your life be guided at
each and every moment of your life.

God wants you to be Rich and Prosperous.

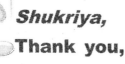

Shukriya,
Thank you,
Thank you,
Thank you,
Dhanyavad...

There are moments in one's life when even words fail to express deep-felt feelings of the heart. I know that this is one such moment in my life, to express gratitude to the many known and also the unknown hearts and minds. It is like capturing the captivating reflection of the full moon in all its glory in a small bowl of water.

A whack on my head

A great Zen Master once called his most intimate disciple suddenly in the middle of the night. The disciple was meditating outside the Master's house. He came in almost immediately.

The Master said, "I had to call you urgently. All these years, I have been hitting you with my stick. Each time you got whacked, you learned something more on awareness. As I see it, you have reached very close to the ultimate goal. By tomorrow morning you will be a Buddha (the enlightened one). So I have to hit you one last time."

The disciple smiled after hearing his Master's curious wish.

He then bowed down to take the whack. The Master whacked him for the last time.

Deeply overwhelmed, the disciple touched the Master's feet with overflowing tears of gratitude.

The one who awakens you is a Master. I see myself as the disciple who has realized his passion for money. I am nothing more than an instrument in the cathartic process. This book would, however be incomplete, had it not been for the many lovely people around me. I thank them immensely for their encouragement and an occasional whack on my head to awaken me from my slumber.

Sonia Nazreth, Lynne Coren, and J. Kedarnath, I thank you for editing and proof reading this book. You helped me with your thoughts and ideas, to give it a final shape. Without your support, this book would have still remained an unrealized dream.

I must also thank S.Mohan, Hemant Jambhale, Joji Valli and Radha Suresh for going through the manuscript with a magnifying glass to check for typographical errors and proof reading. You have added value to this book with your suggestions and ideas.

Suraja and Vibhu, a big 'Thank you' for muscle testing the book using advanced Kinesiology and Universal Circuiting for cellular consciousness.

I must also thank Akash Shah, R.H. Sharma, Atul Bhave, Deepak Kulkarni, G. Balaji, Kaizad, Krishna Iyer, Krishna Sharma, Mahadev Ambekar, Minakshi Sharma, Rachanna

Sharma, Sampath, Sreedhar, Usha Harayani, Vaishali Varenekar, Viral Manek for their encouragement and constant motivation.

The thousands of participants of my 'Money Workshop', spread across the world have also greatly contributed to my understanding of money. I have honed my craft while interacting with them. I would like to thank them for all the valuable insights, thoughts and ideas that they graciously shared with me. Thank you, one and all.

The very core of my existence – my parents, Mr. V. A. Padmanabhan and Mrs. Brinda Padmanabhan, my sister Anuradha and brother-in-law K.S. Buvaraagan, for being with me in good times and bad. I thank you for your prayers, blessings and support.

Last but certainly not the least, I express my deepest gratitude to all of you, my readers, for having trusted that, *I Love Money* will add value to your life.

Facets
of Money

- Are You the Candle?

- Are You the Doormat?

- Power of NO

- How Do We Get Manipulated?

- Crib and You Will Have More Real Situations to Crib

- Complacency Is the Biggest Stumbling Block to Money

- Is Your Money Built on a Foundation of Sacrifice?

- When Death Gives You a Report Card of Life

- Has Your Photograph Appeared in the Obituary Column?

8 Money — Personal Powers   181-199

- Survival of the Toughest

- Power of Being I-centric

- Power of Receiving

- Ask and You Will Receive

- Power of Giving

9 Money — Spending and Saving   201-222

- Do You have Prosperity Eyes?

- Bite into the Wonders of a Juicy Golden Mango

- The Menu Card Mentality

- All I Want Is Everything

- Principle of Maximum Extraction

- Bargain to Glory

- The World Is Out to Give You Money

- There Are Many Idiots at the Top
- The One-man Army
- It Is Time to Buy a Big Fat Lock
- Money and Your Magical Touch
- When Being Small Is Actually Great

Conclusion

The Moon or the Finger

Experience it Live

One Book One Hope

Money Consciousness

Your Own Success Story

Foreword by Money

Most forewords are written by eminent personalities. But, personalities keep coming and going while I'm perhaps a constant factor in this constantly changing world. Think about it, would you even want me to non-existent? Yes, my forms may change but my essence will not. I would like to clarify some misconceptions about myself — home truths, which ought to be known, recognized, understood and applied. I have chosen Suresh Padmanabhan as a medium and through him, I am going to communicate some amazing aspects and secrets about myself to all of you.

This is just the beginning. I will keep connecting back to you very often through his E-books/Cd's, books, lectures and workshops. There are lots of things unsaid, secrets unspoken, mysteries still waiting to be discovered. Your own consciousness will keep discovering more and more secrets in due course.

This young author is quite gifted, not only has he written the book brilliantly but he also believes it to be a bestseller. Some of you will find yourself being disturbed more and more by what you read. The mistakes you made in the past may be reflected quite clearly. Mentally, it will be a different story. You will find yourself reading on and on... You will be tempted to add many insights as you read. The strange beauty of Suresh's work is that it gets you 'involved' pleasantly. It is the stark truth of life seen from a powerful perspcctive.

And what is the expected outcome of reading and getting involved? Personally, you will feel awakened as though from a deep slumber. The steps that you will take henceforth, in the money world will be full of awareness and confidence. This book promises to open newer horizons for you and equips you with the skills necessary to conquer them!

I know you love me but by the time you have read this book, you will also respect me. My guess is that you are going to love reading *I Love Money* and also Suresh, if you get a chance to meet him. He is passionate, not just about me, but also about making a difference in the world. He loves people and wants them to love me as much as he does.

At one point, I discovered that there was more to me than you knew about. Though I have been in your life for a long time, you hardly know me. Even if you think you know me, you know misconstrued by the beliefs floating around about me. Take another look at me and you will realize the potential and power of truth. For a long time I have been silent; I won't be any longer. "The truth shall prevail — Know the truth, speak the truth, share the truth and the truth shall set you free."

Your friend always,

Money.

Let's Start with.... the End!

How would life be if you knew the end at the start? So at the very start I want to give you a framework within which the whole book can be read. Thus, from the very first page you can start getting results, which is the main intention of this book. Read on:

It was a hot summer day and a group was traveling across a desert. One of the group members got separated from the group. Alone, weary and really scared, he dragged his feet in the sand and was almost losing consciousness due to lack of water. He could almost see his end coming towards him. Suddenly, he saw a hand pump and slowly moved towards it. He was very happy to see a glass filled with water. When he was about to drink the water, he noticed a small board on which was written, "This is a magical glass of water, so don't drink this water. Pour the water into the valve of the hand pump. Wait for a moment and when you pump, you will have a lot of water coming through the hand pump."

The poor man had never faced such a terrible dilemma before. What was he to do? A much-needed glass of water in his hand seemed more priceless than the abundant water under the ground. But something made him pour the water as instructed. He started to pump. 1-2-3 no water, he began to curse himself. 4-5-6, again no water, he cursed the person who had written the silly instruction. All of a sudden, he heard a gurgling gush and lo and behold! There was sparkling water pouring in abundance from the hand pump. He drank to his heart's content and also filled some for his journey.

He also filled the glass with water as instructed, otherwise the miracle would stop. As he turned to leave, he paused and went back to the board where all the instructions were written, took a chalk and wrote just two words **"This Works!"**

Not all have the courage to take risks. Henceforth people would never doubt its reliability and the magic would continue forever.

Friends, I am the person who drank the first glass of techniques and was convinced that these 'Techniques Work'. I went on to share this amazing treasure of knowledge with thousands of people all over the world. The participants of my 'Money Workshops' became confident about dealing with money and transformed into happier individuals.

I'm certain that, like them, you too will discover the same conclusion that the 'Techniques Work'. My best wishes are always with you. But let me remind you: For these techniques to work, you have to....... WORK!

Introduction

"If you live life with a smile on your face and song in your heart, you will be able to live happily and welcome success and abundant wealth into your home."

The beauty of the title *I Love Money* is its straightforwardness. *I Love Money* makes no bones about our love for money. It depicts the very foundation of what should be our true relationship with money.

As you keep repeating *I Love Money*, it starts acting as an affirmation in itself to penetrate a deeper essence of love and money into your being.

Say with Pride *I Love Money* every single day and you will find it as attractive and as precious.

This book begins with three activity pages that need to be filled out with a fair amount of excitement and interest. Do follow the given instructions if you wish to get the best out of this book. From then on, every time you open it, you will realize that, it is only when **Money, Personal Powers and a Greater Force** work in sync, do you experience a more fulfilling, harmonic and balanced growth in life.

There are many techniques and formulae in this book that have been tried and tested as part of my Money Workshops. So it makes your life easier as you need not reinvent the wheel.

You will get the best results from this book only if you first shed preconceived (and mostly incorrect!) notions about Money.

Surely, you can't wear a new dress without removing the one you're wearing, can you!!

Read the book from start to end, and then you can read any of the chapter you like, as each chapter is independent. As you read, please keep a pen/pencil ready so that you can write down your own ideas and thoughts. You will get many ideas pertaining to money and to your life as you keep reading this book regularly. Each time you read it, you will gain fresh insight by seeing things from a different perspective.

Read the book a number of times. Keep it by your bedside or carry it with you so you can read the book consistently for a minimum of 21 days which is the minimum number of days required to uproot weak habits and substitute it with strong habits.

Your friends will want to borrow *I Love Money*. Be forewarned they won't return it back to you. So it would be a great idea to gift your friends a copy of *I Love Money*.

There are many ideas in this book which you will just love and agree with because, for you, it would be more of a re-affirmation of your own thoughts. At times, you will think differently and might not accept some of the ideas put forth — fair enough. You simply have to learn how to apply these thoughts to your own life to get the best results out of this book.

Let the thoughts from *I Love Money* be a spring board to 'Actions'. Only 'Actions' will get the money flowing into your wallet and ensure you quality in your life.

If reading this book makes a difference in your life, do recommend it to your friends and relatives. Your blessings and recommendations will help to spread the consciousness of money around the world. I thank you in advance for your caring and sharing.

Do attend the Money Workshops which are a natural extension of this book and will benefit you immensely.

Say 'Yes to Money'

"T'is money that makes the world go round!" goes the famous saying about money. Quite true isn't it? Money does make the world go round. If its not in your pocket, its in your head. A part of everybody's life, a part of you, that's what money is. It has such great power that it can command attention from everyone.

Try a simple experiment to know its power. Drop a couple of coins in any place where its magical tinkle can be heard. And you can feel time itself freezing. People around you, stop right where they are stop whatever they may be doing, and look in the direction where they heard money's magical sound. Almost instantaneously they wonder if it was their money that had dropped.

Some may even rattle their pockets, in spite of not having any loose coins there. Were the coin to roll under a table, people may even forget they have lumbago and look for it there.

Scarcity Mentality — The Need for the Magic Hat

All human beings desire to be rich and prosperous. God wants all his creations to experience abundance at all times. Yet, somewhere along the way some of us have lost the ability to tune in with blessings of abundance. Happiness and prosperity always seem a step away from us and a little out of reach.

Who told us that resources in nature are scarce?

I invite you to a discovery. Drop the old hat of 'scarcity' and wear the 'magic hat' that has the secrets of abundance woven into its fabric. These secrets are right there waiting for you to explore them. So come along and live a life full of wisdom, beauty, truth and love.

Lights, Camera, Action

The Fire-Eating Experience

How would you react if asked to eat a piece of burning cotton? Forget about eating it, you wouldn't even want to come close to one!

And what if I were to demonstrate eating burning cotton (we do this at times as part of The Money Workshop). Somewhere a doubt will arise in your mind, "If someone can do it, why can't I?" Slowly, there begins a transition from an attitude of 'impossible' to 'possible'. Possibility is notional and remains only in your mind. This can become a reality only if you actually eat the burning cotton.

Now you decide to learn how to eat burning cotton. Just mere learning would not suffice, as this would still be the *Knowing State*. To create your own personal experience, you actually need to take the necessary steps and perform the action thus going into the *Doing State*.

So you finally decide to take up the challenge. (Warning: Do not attempt this on your own. People performing this act are trained professionals.) As you attempt this experiment of putting the burning cotton in your mouth you will encounter great fear. The greater the fear the more difficult is the task.

Finally you are able to eat the burning cotton without any harm. You feel elated and triumphant. You have won over your own fears and experience a sense of victory. The second time is far easier and now the fear of eating burning cotton has eliminated from your life forever.

This stage is called an *Achievement Stage*. If you had chosen technically to understand how to eat burning cotton, but had never attempted the same, so just knowing is not enough. We must use and apply the knowledge to make it happen. Facing a challenge and actually 'doing' the action is a step towards strengthening of the mind by killing the 'fear demons'.

When you take action you empower yourself.

The process is the same be it eating burning cotton, investing for the first time in the stock market or taking a new decision regarding money or finances.

You will have to pass the following stages: First, the stage of impossibility, then stage of possibility (presently only in the mind). The third stage is that of action or the Doing Stage (where you will encounter tremendous doubt or fear), and finally to reach the Achievement Stage (after successfully having created your own personal experience).

The inability or fear of taking actions is what actually hinders one's progress. Therefore, attempt baby steps in the right direction. Even if you fail it will be worthwhile, for you would have learned from that failure, things which will be valuable all through your life. So, become action-oriented. Remember, every monument started with one stone. And, no money was or will ever be made without necessary actions in that direction.

Please etch it clearly in your minds that,

'Knowing is not doing. Only actual doing is doing.'

The
Importance
of Money

The fastest way to attract money is love money, love people and love yourself

— Suresh Padmanabhan

Circulate and play the game of money joyfully.

The Perplexing and Baffling World of Money

The biggest Money Rule, all who have Money make the rules.

— Suresh Padmanabhan

Some of the costliest paintings running into millions of dollars were created by the master artist Vincent van Gogh. You will be surprised to know that the this person lived and died in austerity?

There are innumerable such stories of people who have worked hard all through their lives. They stack away millions of dollars or rupees and lead a miserly life never spending money even on themselves. Then, before they know it, they're too old and sick to enjoy that wealth. They make all their millions and one fine day they give it all to charity.

There are others who resort to crime and fraud to make fast money. They succumb to the lure of money and do not mind taking an unfair route to make money. They steal, cheat, even kill near and dear ones for the sake of money.

There is a gap between the rich and the poor who can barely

afford to make two ends meet: While the rich take even their pets to beauty parlours and buy them designer collars, millions die hungry and homeless on the streets.

There are a few who make millions in a single day, while there are millions who make only few rupees each day.

There are many who with their entire wealth still feel insecure and there are those who even with less money feel like emperors.

There are many who don't get sleep even on the most expensive quilt beds and others who sleep like logs on the hardest of benches and rocks.

There are rags-to-riches stories which inspire us and there are also riches to rags stories which startle and perplex us.

The world is a strange place to live, with all its contrasts. We live in a degree world where the range is from one end to the other extreme. Whatever you thought or could not even think will exist somewhere on this planet. There is no end to worries but we must learn to let go of certain problems and tensions if we are to live our life in happiness. As they say, Money is a good slave but a bad master. This means that you must learn to make money work for you rather than allow it to rule your life and thoughts.

Therefore, it is best that you are only bothered with yourself and are choosy with what you want to connect in the world of Money.

Can You Buy the Starry Night?

Without Money life will be like a flower without fragrance, a sun without rays, a bird without wings, the earth without atmosphere, and a human being without blood.

— *Suresh Padmanabhan*

Have you ever seen the night sky closely? A spectacular carpet of stars besides a singular moon glitters throughout the night to give way to the rising Sun at dawn. Our Earth is also one of God's most wonderful and beautiful creations. Gushing waterfalls, towering mountains, dense forests and the rich and colourful flora and fauna make for a truly fantastic picture. It is as though the entire cosmos has put up a 'sound and light' spectacle and a live orchestra just for us free of cost. Remember some of the best things in life still come free.

How many of us take time to enjoy and appreciate this beauty? Do we stop to catch the last glimpses of a setting Sun or steal some moments to go and see it rise on the horizon? Don't we take all this for granted? What if an administrator comes from the heaven to collect a sunlight tax or a full moon tax or a starlit night tax? It is time to wake up and look at the grandeur on display — available for all of us and yet free! God has been kind to us... let him not regret it.

Even Money Couldn't Help Him Out...

Mr. Malamaal goes to the beach with his wife. On the way he stops to pick some snacks, upon his return he is shocked to see his wife being pulled out of the water. People around are trying to revive the unconscious lady. He asks what they are doing, to which they reply "We are giving artificial respiration."

Malamaal screams: "Artificial! "Hell," give her the real thing. I will pay for it!"

Abundance and prosperity apply to money and go much beyond. On the material level, it is more of fulfillment of one's needs, wants and desires. Abundance would mean not having to worry about lack of money or wealth, simply because there's more than enough of it. One would then be able to enjoy the wealth that one has inherited or created.

On the spiritual sphere, abundance and prosperity would mean richness of the soul. When you have deep and intense connectivity both, within your own 'Self' as well as with the Universe, you are truly prosperous and in a state of total abundance. You live in the 'now' and enjoy it with the innocence of a child.

On the mental sphere, abundance is 'security' and 'content-ment'. A person who is truly prosperous on the mental level has peace of mind and experiences bliss in every single moment. He/she lives in eternal happiness unbounded, infinite and unlimited. It is having frequent moments with feelings of internal vastness and richness. It is leading a meaningful life in harmony with existence.

This infinite abundance transports you to a new dimension where life is no more black and white but brilliant and truly melodious. It is only when you connect with existence on these varied levels, with intensity and passion you can truly say "I am rich and prosperous."

So money is not simply confined to crisp currency notes and just not in your wallet, it is all around. Let us explore the complete journey of Money from here towards abundance and prosperity.

Temporary and Permanent Solutions

Acquaintance: A person whom we know well enough to borrow from, but not well enough to lend to.

— Ambrose Bierce

While we encounter different kinds of monetary problems, there are only three ways of handling them. The first is that you do not work out a solution and simply pray that God takes care of it. The second is that you work out a temporary solution that will take care of the current problem. The last way to handle a monetary problem is of course, to go to the root of the problem and work out a permanent solution to it.

Golmaal was in a fix. He needed Rs 10,000 badly and did not know whom to ask. He approached his friend, Malamaal for a loan. "I promise to return the money in a month" he said. But, like the money, his promises also vanished into thin air. Now, Malamaal started getting worried about getting his money back. To get rid of his constant pestering, Golmaal approached Dhaniram, a friend with whom he had not been in touch for ages. He made the same request and the same promise to the unsuspecting Dhaniram and managed to get Rs. 10,000 from him as well. After getting Rs. 10,000 from Dhaniram he went straight and handed it over to Malamaal. He heaved a sigh of relief now that he had managed to return his debt. Another month went by and it was time to pay back Dhaniram. By now Golmaal had discovered a nice solution.

Golmaal ran back to Malamaal and asked him again for Rs. 10,000 which he promised to return in a month's time. Malamaal now trusted his friend to return his money and thus lent him the money willingly. Golmaal gave this money to Dhaniram. Golmaal figured out that he was not just making things work well for him, he was keeping both his creditors happy too!

Month after month, he kept taking from one to return the other's debt. However, fraud does not have a very long life and soon, Golmaal became a victim of his own devise. He got confused as to who he had borrowed from and whom he had to return. He did not know whether to take the Rs. 10,000 from Dhaniram to give to Malamaal or vice versa. He got rather tired and wanted to solve this issue permanently. He called them over for tea. He introduced Malamaal and Dhaniram to each other. When they were about to leave, he simply said, "I have to thank you both for having lent me money. But now, it is getting quite confusing, having to deal with the two of you. Do me a favour, just keep exchanging Rs. 10,000/- between the two of you every month!"

The friends were appalled, to say the least!!

Many of us solve our money problems like Golmaal. Borrow from here, give there. Take profits from one running business and invest in some other business that is making losses. But we need to understand that these are nothing but temporary solutions. They will raise their ugly heads at some point or the other. The vicious circle would thus go on and on, never letting you get out of the clutches of financial problems.

The ancient Indian system of Ayurveda had a permanent solution to good health and vitality. Ayurvedic medicines worked on principle of prevention of disease rather than its cure. And why would a healthy person feel the need for any medication?

Your vehicle requires maintenance on regular basis to keep it in a good condition. Of course, there are special circumstances when you do experience a sudden problem. The key here is to pre-empt the problem and keep a solution ready in such a situation. For example, if you have a flat tyre in the middle of a busy road, you must be well-equipped with necessary tools and a spare tyre to fix the problem there and then. As a proactive measure, you would also get regular servicing and checks done.

One does not have any control on natural disasters and calamities like war, earthquakes, riots or recession. Such incidents have uprooted entire lives of people. Such incidents can also severely affect our financial health. Nevertheless, we must learn to rise and survive such situations. We must follow some simple money management rules that are in tune with natural laws, doing this will result in toning up our 'financial muscle' and see us through a financial crisis.

Saving early is a good habit, its a skill. Having good reserves can help in difficult times. One therefore needs to cultivate the 'savings' habit early on in life. If you observe carefully, you will notice that certain sections of people remain more or less unaffected in times of general economic catastrophe. It is this habit that helps them face difficult times.

So it does make a lot of sense to follow footsteps that subscribe to the philosophy of prevention rather than cure. Keeping aside money for unexpected problems, old age and your children's further education are habits that truly 'pay off' in the long run.

You're Dead without Money

Money is the barometer of a society's virtue.

— *Ayn Rand*

The biggest lie you have ever heard is, "Money is not important in my life." There is enough proof that whatever you are today and whatever you will ever be is shaped by money. And it is pointless to deny the role that money plays in one's life.

Everything you are today is an outcome of the money flow in your life — your status, net worth, and self-image. You do need money to buy necessities, wants and sometimes, even luxuries. Money is the fuel that keeps the cycle of life moving. You run out of it and your cycle stops!

Money is perhaps as essential as the air you breathe, as vital as a mother's milk is to her new-born baby or as life-giving as the blood circulating in your body. Whether you love it or hate it, you simply cannot live without money.

Friend: "I need your advice friend. It is a question of life and death."

Golmal: "Don't worry, I am good at giving advice. Tell me, what is your problem?"

Friend: "Should I marry the one-eyed widow who is a millionaire or the pretty girl who is very poor or the pretty penniless girl whom I am in love with?"

Golmal: "Friend, trust your heart. What does your heart say?"

Friend: "You have opened my eyes; money is not everything in the world. I want to marry the girl whom I love even though she is poor."

Golmal: "Good! Always trust your heart, brother. By the way, now that you have decided to marry the poor girl, please give me the phone number of the one-eyed widow!"

If you think that money is important only from birth to death then you are wrong. Remember that even funerals are not free though you are not the one paying for them.

Make an important decision here and now. Do you really want money or not? If yes, you'll have to be very clear to value its importance. Money presents itself only to those who deeply value and cherish it.

Why I hate Money?

Never run away from Money for you will regret when Money will run away from you.

— Suresh Padmanabhan

While I was in Russia for a book-signing event a very upset looking lady came towards me. Pointedly looking at me she said, "You are speaking and writing about evil."

I was astounded and said, "Sorry Madam, Could you please repeat what you said?"

She repeated angrily," You are speaking and writing about evil."

I replied, "No, you are mistaken, I write and speak about Money."

"Yes," she said triumphantly, "That is exactly what I am saying. Money is evil, very evil!"

"Do you really think so?" I asked.

"Yes." She emphasized, "Yes, yes, yes, and very, very evil."

I smiled and said, "Then, please give me all your evil. I will gladly accept it and liberate you from evil. And yes, the more evil you give me the more happier we both will be!"

Suddenly there was complete silence and the lady just disappeared from that place.

One hears such talks everywhere. Sometimes unknowingly even you must have spoken in a similar vein. Worldwide there is more hate for money than love. People who have money hate it and people who do not have money hate it more. Why do we have such a hypocritical attitude towards money?

In India we have innumerable anti-money proverbs such as "Money is like dirt", "Money ruins life", "Money comes and goes, so why bother" and so on. Harboring such thoughts creates a negative shield in your mind that pushes money away from your life.

Decide now, Do you want Money for your life?

I am sure the answer is yes. Then why be a hypocrite? Become conscious and aware of not harboring such thoughts in your mind.

Golmal was trying to push out a piece of heavy luggage but since it was very heavy it got stuck in the doorway. So he sought his neighbor's help. His neighbor came along and was confident that he would solve this problem. He asked Golmal to go inside of the door and he took a position outside the door. Both of them started pushing with force.

After a lot of screaming, ranting, gasping, the luggage had not moved a single inch. Golmal got tired and sweating all over screamed what the hell." I have been trying to push out the luggage with all my strength and it has hardly moved".

His neighbor sheepishly said oops" I thought the luggage was to be pushed inside".

When you apply two equal forces opposing each other then there can be no movement in either direction. When you take hot water and mix it with cold water and keep mixing hot and cold water, the water neither becomes hot nor cold. In a game of tug-of-war, if both sides are equally strong, there is much effort but no movement.

Similarly when you hate money, how do you expect the energy of money to be nice to you?

Nobody Loves You When You Don't Have Money

That money talks
I'll not deny.
I heard it once:
It said, 'Goodbye.'

— *Richard Armour*

Let's go back to a time in your life when you had that 'money-crisis'. Can you recollect the nagging worry, tension and frustration? Did you really feel good about yourself? You did not. This is the stark truth and you know it deep down. You were at your lowest self-esteem. You may have seen that peculiar look friends and relatives gave you. And remember the admonitions from all the people on how to run your life better?

Golmaal to his friend: "Could you lend me some money. I want to buy a tiger to guard my house."

Friend: "What! You have practically nothing in your house and yet want to guard it. My advice to you is become rich first, then keep a tiger."

Golmaal: "I asked you for money and not advice."

Haven't you desperately wished for a place where you could really 'cash in' all that advice with 'real currency?'

Then came the crash, money got sucked and the going got tough. Your friends disappeared just like your money. You experienced feelings of helplessness, hurt and anger.

Forget friends; look at your own shadow. When the sun is shining brightly, your shadow follows you so faithfully. When it is dark, your shadow too disappears. Without Money you realize that 'you are a non-entity.'

When things go wrong with finances, we try to determine the causes. We feel that we probably miscalculated certain monetary decisions. Perhaps we delayed certain important steps. We try to rewind and relive all the steps. Everything that seemed correct at that point seems to have gone wrong now. We hate our own self for the consequences. We seem to be unforgiving.

You will whole-heartedly agree with the well-known stanza!

"Laugh and the world laughs with you,

Weep and you weep alone...

Feast and your halls are crowded,

Fast and the world goes by..."

At such times, one sees an odd mathematical logic where,

'Disappearance of friends is directly proportional to disappearance of money.'

It is said "success has many fathers but failure is an orphan." The bitter truth you need to face is that you were hurt because you did not understand the value of money.

Now, imagine yourself strolling in a shopping mall with your wallet bulging with money. Your face will regain the natural glow bestowed on you from birth. The way you walk, the way you talk, in short, everything about you has the aura and radiance. Money is enough to give you a powerful magnetic personality. Do you need anything else to enhance your personality?

Money has a powerful impact on everything around you. Recognize the value and importance of Money at all times.

Why Are We So Uncomfortable with Money?

One of the biggest lies in the world is "Money is not important in my life"

— Suresh Padmanabhan

"Do you love me Golmaal?" asked the cute girl.

"Of course I do, sweetheart" he replied.

"When will you marry me then?" she asked.

"Oh! No, let us not change the subject" Golmaal replied.

We behave in exactly the same way, when it comes to talking about "money" We do not enjoy talking about money and so, we simply change the topic. Why is it that we are able to speak at length and with great ease on every topic except money? It often is a taboo area and there is a hesitation to discuss money even with near and dear ones.

Right from childhood to old age, life is full of experiences and relationships. We also find money playing a very important role in shaping our personality. Money is entwined with all relationships, aspirations and the reality of your being. Why then is it so difficult to talk about money?

Shying away from school fees will not reduce the fees nor change the last date. Life's cruel realities do not make exceptions for anyone. In business dealings, people discuss products and services very enthusiastically. But when you need to inform about the price you start feeling very conscious about yourself, and find it very difficult to talk about it.

People work very hard but when it comes to asking for what is due to them, they hesitate in asking for the same. When it comes to asking for a salary that you know you deserve, you just hesitate and never manage to ask. But friends, it is better and important that you demand your rightful salary. Attach both, value and importance to what you offer, and must rightfully get what you feel you deserve

What a strange state of affairs! We are comfortable having money problems but become uncomfortable while confronting them. Why do people go through life carrying the burden of discomfort with money all the time? Terrible misconceptions about money have been forced upon us over the years. And now, money has become an uncomfortable five letter word.

Psychiatrist to Money Bags: "Don't worry Money Bags we all have problems. Look I too have problems."

"I will solve your problems in 20 sittings" and "I will charge Rs 1000 per session."

Money Bags: "That sure solves your problem, Doc! What about mine?"

The bottom-line is — "It is your money." Don't shy away from it. Be natural and talk straight when it comes to money, always.

Understanding Money Is Understanding Life

"Every day I get up and look through the Forbes list of the richest people in America. If I'm not there, I go to work."

— Robert Orben

Pull a currency note out of your wallet and take a good look at it. Caress it with love, care, totality and alertness. You can actually see the story of your own life unfold before your eyes. Every currency note or coin tells the fascinating story about you. Every area of our life from relationships to health is deeply entwined with 'Money'. It is very unfortunate that this aspect of our life has been neglected for all this while.

You will agree that, when the money area of our life gets affected, it has a snowball effect on the other areas of our lives. Money is a very special mirror that shows us the reality and truth of our lives, exactly like it is. And if needed, you can use it to tidy yourself up and get things done for you.

Our feelings always reflect our current 'Money Position'. Imagine you just have had a hard day at work and you return home, tired. Just as you are settling down, you switch on the TV. The life styles of the rich and famous is being telecast. Your wife while serving tea casually informs that the cable man has hiked the rate. Just then door bell rings, and there is your friendly neighbour and family. They have come to distribute sweets for their purchase of a brand new car. But since you have diabetes, you cannot have a piece. Your reactions, behaviour and relationship with everyone can be anybody's guess!

Most of us take things for granted when we have them. It is the same with money too. Our wallet, for example, is not cause for much concern as long as it is in our pocket. Lose it and our world turns upside down. When there is little money, we feel the need for some more. And while we have more of it, we feel anxious and insecure that we might end up losing it.

> Friend: "Do you know Malamaal, the rich man died a sudden death. Sadly, he did not leave a single rupee for his children."
>
> Golmal: "Yes, I have known him all my life. He led a very imbalanced life. First, he lost his health becoming wealthy and then he lost his wealth becoming healthy."

So friends, please steer clear from the cobwebs of confusion in understanding your relationship with money. It would be disastrous to attempt solving problems in isolation such as tackling a liver problem here or a relationship problem there. Start by acknowledging that money is a bottle-neck area in life. Start caring for money, treat it with a lot of love and respect. Be genuinely interested about your money. Resolving problems in this domain could lead you to finding long-term solutions to these. And just like the truth that the neck of any bottle is always closer to its top than the bottom — it is the truth that bottleneck areas of money are in your own head. Disentangle the 'money knots' and you will find other problem areas clearing themselves up automatically.

As your money area flourishes, your life too will flourish like a garden full of fresh flowers.

Money and Sticking to Basics

The only reason a great many American families don't own an elephant is that they have never been offered an elephant for a dollar down and easy weekly payments.

— Mad Magazine

Pay attention to Money or You will 'Pay' for it.

Towards or Away from Money

A business that makes nothing but money is a poor business.

— Henry Ford

There are only two pathways of money. Many of us just keep rushing through life blindfoldedly, giving no or very little thought to our actions. We must remember that every action of ours has the potential to take us, either towards money or away from it. Being aware of the two paths is nothing less than an eye-opener. If you have been handling money mechanically, like a currency counting machine then you can be sure of some danger lurking nearby.

For example, many of us delay taking money decisions. You all may have heard the wise saying that **"Procrastination is the thief of time."** I would like to change that to say, **"Procrastination is the thief of both, your money and time."** The funny part is that you keep postponing issues that need your priority. Putting off monetary issues to a later date takes you deeper into the clutches of a monetary crisis.

Being lazy and ignorant about the money world, being disorganized, not keeping proper accounts, not being bothered about money, escaping from current monetary issues are some of the blunders that people make. And then despite this self-created mess, they foolishly curse the world when they do not get what is rightfully due to them. This book contains clear insights into such issues. People must however understand that, to get the right results you have to do the right things in the right manner and at the right time.

It is essential for you to realize that 'actions come first and Money only follows.' Wrong actions can never lead to right results and right actions can never lead to wrong results. Learn that the money world we create is like a castle built on the strong foundations of action.

You are now the captain of your own ship. It is therefore up to you, to steer your ship towards success, prosperity and money.

Start Early onto Your Journey of Money

"Ordinary riches can be stolen; real riches cannot. In your soul are infinitely precious things that cannot be taken from you."

— Oscar Wilde

Money impressions are formed very early in life. Some of the belief systems of money can be embedded as early as in the womb. Some of the most vital years of our life are between 0 to 7 years. Now you would be wondering can it be so early.

Read the experiment conducted with full awareness:

The Marshmallow experiment by Prof Walter Mischel

The Stanford Marshmallow Experiment was a study on deffered gratification conducted by Prof. Walter Mischel in the year 1972, at Stanford University, California.

He studied a group of four-year-old children, each of whom

was given one marshmallow the condition was if the child could resist eating the marshmallow for 20 minutes, then the child would be given a second marshmallow as a gift for waiting. Some children were able to wait the twenty minutes, and some were unable to wait. Furthermore, the university researchers then studied the developmental progress of each participant child into adolescence, and reported that children able to delay gratification (wait) were psychologically better adjusted, more dependable persons, and as high school students, scored significantly greater grades in the collegiate Scholastic Aptitude Test. They turned out to be better human beings.

Children who passed the marshmallow test enjoyed greater success as adults. While the children who gave in to temptation were found to be under stress and no self control as adults, our inherent qualities become habit by repetition. So we need to become aware of our weaknesses and strengths at an early age.

Teach your children the value of Money and the virtues of saving, healthy habits, conscious spending, and other traits that will add value to their life as they grow. Sow the seeds early to reap the fruits later in life.

The Game Plan for Money

It isn't necessary to be rich and famous to be happy. it's only necessary to be rich.

— *Alan Alda*

Take a look at our 'serious' relationship with money. This serious attitude influences the way we behave with money. Life is not that grim as we may be led to believe.

It was past midnight but Golmaal just could not sleep. He was twisting and turning in the bed.

Mrs. Golmaal got very disturbed looking at her husband and asked him what the problem was. Golmaal was tense because he had borrowed a lakh of rupees, a year ago from Seth Malamaal and had promised to repay him soon. The day had arrived but Golmaal had made no such arrangements. Naturally, he was worried of the consequences.

Mrs. Golmaal picked up the phone and called up Seth

Malamaal at midnight. After many rings Seth Malamaal asked in a sleepy voice who was it.

Mrs. Golmaal: "I am Mrs. Golmaal and my husband had borrowed a lakh of rupees from you last year. He had also promised to pay you back the money by tomorrow."

Seth Malamaal: "Oh! Yes I am eagerly waiting for the money."

Mrs Golmaal: "Let me tell you now itself that my husband has made no arrangement for the money so he won't be able to pay you." So saying, she banged down the phone.

After that Golmaal felt much better and slept well while Seth Malamaal now was turning and twisting in bed.

In a lighter vein, we learn the importance of being playful and relaxed. *'Be aware'* should be the motto for a joyful life and that includes money. It is not *be ware* and forever be tense.

A game is an enjoyable activity that engages the mind and body along with some natural phenomenon. With gravity, for example, you throw something up and it comes down. All children and many of you find joy in the activity of throwing a ball up and catching it while coming down. The whole activity is a game. The ball, you, your action and the forces of nature are interacting playfully and there is natural joy as a result.

You hit a ball with a bat and it crashes through a neighbour's window. You have got your six but are in a fix. That kind of a shot is stadium class. It deserves an open playground and applauding spectators. Playing such a shot in the street or in your backyard is nothing short of an invitation to trouble.

Money too is a natural phenomenon. Being playful with money

is when you can see money and enjoy its natural beauty. But to play the game, you ought to know and follow its rules. As in any other game, the vital elements in the money game are clear knowledge of the game rules and skill of the players. Like an artisan, you must polish your skills regularly to improve your quality of work. With your skills, your success will increase by leaps and bounds. Throughout this book you will come across various rules of 'money' which you can skillfully master. From today you can be very serious or start playing the game of Money everyday of your life.

In the Game of Money and Life,
every Opportunity Matters.

Would You like to Tear Up Currency?

When you let money speak for you, it drowns out anything else you meant to say.

— Mignon McLaughlin,

Just try a small experiment. Take a currency note from your wallet (higher denominations are better). Fold it into half and then tear it neatly along the fold line. Stack those two halves. Fold them again into half and tear it...By now, you must be thinking I have gone crazy. Why would I want to tear up my own money? Isn't it a stupid and disgraceful act? Who in his right state of mind would do that? Why should you not tear currency notes? Contemplate on the reasons why you should not. Write them down.

One of the main reasons you will come up is that the currency note loses its value. Have you ever willingly torn money in your life? I'm sure you have never done so. But it does not qualify as a just answer simply because you must have lost money at some point or the other. The number of times you have lost money or wasted it is no different from tearing it apart. If you calculate how much you have torn and thrown away, it would run into hundreds of thousands.

Money when put to use has the potential to grow. Therefore, when you waste money, you not only destroy it, but also cut out the possibility of its growth. It stops being of any use to you as well as bringing you more and more of itself into your life.

When you deposit your money as savings in a bank, they pay you interest on it. You are respected by everyone therefore being a customer of the bank. Bank managers even welcome you into their cabin and treat you with utmost courtesy. The amount of money you have saved with the bank determines (to some extent), the love and respect you command there.

There is nothing in the world that cannot be rectified. You must learn from your past mistakes and avoid repeating them if you really want to move up the money ladder. Do ask yourself often, "Is careless action with money equivalent to tearing it up?" Just being in an alert and aware state is enough to ensure that you will not tear the currency. Once this is done, learn to extend this awareness to all money transactions.

Forgetfulness Is the Worst Human Disease

The easiest thing to do with Money-
"Spend it". Every fool can.

— Suresh Padmanabhan

Take a look at our ancient scriptures, you will realize that the most terrifying 'curse' was the one that took away the knowledge or power of a particular skill, at that moment when it was needed the most. Forgetfulness remains to be a curse even today.

Making rules and regulations is not a daunting task at all. To adhere to the rules and regulations is. We know how easy it is to break them. The thing is if you break a rule or regulation in the money world, you are punished, often not by somebody but the situation itself. **Just like the man who burns his right cheek with a hot iron thinking it's the phone and then proceeds to commit the same folly the next day thereby burning his left cheek.**

Vehicles are driven on the right side of the road in USA. In most of the countries, they keep to the left. Imagine your much planned visit to the USA is a reality. How dangerous it would be for you to forget you are in America and drive on the wrong side?

In every person's life, there are money-related instances when he/she has been forgetful. Do you remember the restaurant you went to along with friends? The hefty bill and spending was beyond your means. You came home a little sad and swore to be careful with your money. But you simply forget this vow the very next day!

Who doesn't like to receive payments? But how many of us promptly deposit the cheques we receive in the bank? You tend to forget to pay your bills on time and end up paying a surcharge on it. On the way back home you forget to buy the groceries. You are forced to go back all the way wasting time and money for the same task. Believe me, bad habits are really easy to form and forgetfulness is nothing different. It can prove to be quite detrimental to your financial health.

We forget a thing simply because our mind has not given it enough importance to be remembered. Money and financial matters are of prime importance and should not be treated as trivial. This includes not 'forgetting' the natural laws of money. How fortunate that you have learnt to co-exist with gravity. Otherwise imagine the consequence of jumping out of a tall building — forgetting what gravity is all about!

Yes, it is human to err. If life indeed were to be a process of learning from mistakes, you rather make new mistakes every day and learn. It is better than making the same mistake again and again and yet not learn. You simply have to stay away from vicious cycles of money errors.

Please remember not to be forgetful!

The Ultimate Purpose of Money

Money doesn't make you happy. I now have $50 million but I was just as happy when I had $48 million.

— Arnold Schwarzenegger

Answer this simple question. "Why do you want to earn money?" The answers could be to afford things for our survival, comfort, to experience freedom, to be successful and so on. Now, if you were asked, "Why do you want to be comfortable or be successful?" The answers will again be different for different people. If I were to go on with a string of 'why's', the final answer would be, "because I want to be happy." You will eventually realize that man's ultimate goal behind earning more and more money is to afford things that would make him/her happy.

What if I were then to ask, "When will you be happy?", Some may answer, "When my house is built" while for some others it would be a good job.

As a short exercise, do pause for a moment, reflect and ponder over your answer because it will reveal many secrets of your inner self. You will understand whether your happiness depends upon certain external conditions that are fulfilled. This is nothing but a mirage desert oasis, the closer you get, the further away it seems. Similarly, when you reach a particular goal that you think would make you happy, you will see that it has actually transformed into another goal post far from you. And so, you keep running after it, for your entire life seeking that elusive happiness.

If you notice the faces of many rich people, you might wonder why they look unhappy or strangely dejected, despite having enough and more. The happiness quotient is completely missing from their life. They may flash their diamonds and drive their swanky cars, but somehow still look dissatisfied with life. 'Money by itself can do nothing.' It needs you, here and now. It requires a positive attitude. There is no 'after this or that, or when and if this happens' in the Money World.

Let me tell you yet another great secret about money. It has a "multiplier and enlarger effect" in life. It simply enlarges and multiplies your own core emotions. If in your core you have happiness, money multiplies your happiness. If you are, habitually, a 'sad sack', money multiplies your own sadness. Emotions may be in your head, eyes and heart but the controls are in your hands. It is not that she is happy because she is rich. It is, **'She is happy therefore she is rich.'**

Learning from M.O.N.E.Y

When I had money I did not respect it, now I want to respect money, but I don't have any.

— *Suresh Padmanabhan*

Let us learn from the word 'M O N E Y'.

If you look closely, the word 'one' is an integral part of the word 'money'. Embedded in the word money is ONE. It is the smallest unit and smallest value of money. When we realize the value of every single rupee we start becoming money-conscious. As they say, **"Little drops of water and little grains of sand make the mighty ocean and the pleasant land."**

Similarly, every rupee adds up to a huge fortune. Every saving and every loss has its root in the smallest unit of money. If you think a single rupee is insignificant then you develop a wrong and wasteful habit of losing money. It won't be a surprise if you end up losing all your money slowly and steadily. For money to stay with you and grow by leaps and bounds, you ought to value it, love it. Now, valuing every single rupee is not being 'stingy' as wrongly believed. Rather, it has everything to do with us being aware, methodical and always in control. Many a time, bigger problems occur when smaller issues are neglected. The huge Titanic sank because of a small hole in it that was left unplugged.

Never underestimate the power of the single unit, 'One'. When you start saving in units of one, it goes on to become a huge amount. It greatly helps to be an alert person so as to not allow the loss or misuse of even a single unit of your hard-earned money. Please understand that this is not being unduly preoccupied with money. Your awareness and consciousness should be limited to the extent that your money is channelized correctly so as to multiply itself.

There is something intriguing in the world of numbers. There are only two numbers — 0 (zero) and 1 (one). The rest of the numbers are only their combinations. While 0 symbolizes the end, 1 symbolizes a new beginning. Therefore in India, it is considered auspicious to gift money in denominations of Re. 1/- For example, we always gift Rs. 11, Rs. 21 and so on. The reason behind this is to wish him more and more luck by way of money. The extra 1 denotes a new beginning and abundance in wealth.

If you remove the word 'ONE' from Money you get the letters 'M' and 'Y'. Together these form the word 'MY'. The message is loud and clear — "Be concerned only with your money." The problem with many people is that they concern themselves more with other people's problems and financial issues than with their own. We are more curious about the signing amounts of film stars or sports personalities than about what our children are earning. We are like the daily newspapers passing this to others (often with added and imaginary information).

You may be bothered about the national budgets, the national economy, global monetary situations, etc. But, how do you feel about your 'own money?' This money is your own. You can touch and feel it and spend it for your needs and happiness. All the other types, you cannot touch even with a pole. No one is going to part with their money because you are interested in it. Your money is yours. Their money is theirs. Mind your own money and let others mind theirs.

Life Is Simple
Human Beings
Are Not

Money builds spirituality: show me any temple or church built out of just thin air.

— Suresh Padmanabhan

Let me give you an example.

In a multimillion dollar project that was set up to document activity in space, astronauts were sent into space to document their own experiences there. However, it was later discovered that one could not write with ordinary pens in zero gravity conditions.

This was a complex problem. Everyone at the base station was in a flurry with ideas and plans to design a pen that would write in outer space. The young office boy often tried to say something but the 'grey-haired'ignored him. Finally someone took pity on the boy and let him have his say. He said, "Hey, since the Russians went into space before us, why not see what they did?" The Commander sent a fax across asking the Russians how they had managed. Almost instantaneously, the Russians replied, "We used pencils!"

It was that simple. What set the boy apart from the intelligentia was his simple approach and common sense. Solutions sometimes have a knack of being very obvious yet very difficult to spot. What is needed is a change in perspective of the person who is seeking the solution. Solutions to most problems are simple and they can come from the most unexpected and unlikely sources.

Here's another example.

A six-ton machinery equipment was to be placed in a pit at the construction site of a factory. Unfortunately, the crane broke down. It could be fixed only when experts could come from a nearby town in a couple of days. Work at the site came to a standstill. The camp cook-cum-waiter, a jolly old fellow noticed this and casually commented, "Sirs, but why don't you use ice? Here! Have this cold drink and cheer up." Yes, ice it was!

The next day, the workers filled the pit with truckloads of ice and slid the machinery on it. The ice started to melt and the water was pumped out leaving the machinery snug exactly where it was needed! A simple solution wasn't it!

Simplify Money Issues and Simplify Life

If you are a shopkeeper and are fed up with customers bargaining, simply put up a placard that reads, 'Fixed price, no bargaining.' If you are a doctor and patients negotiate on your consultation fees, you could route all the payments through your receptionist. If you are weak in bargaining then you could choose stores where the prices are fixed. Phone companies that got tired of chasing customers who wouldn't pay up came up with a really simple solution. They cut off the line until the customers came and paid up their bills.

Develop a lateral thinking bent of mind. This helps in bringing up simple solutions to problems. Always ask yourself if there is a simpler way of doing a particular task. When you do come up with solutions, do not get engrossed in deep analysis and reasoning. As long as they work for you, they are great. Put them into action and make them workable.

Let us not complicate a simple thing like money and let it destroy the peace and happiness in our life. Money works its way beautifully and enhances the quality of life only when we treat it as important and value its place in our scheme of things.

Money — Perfect Handling and Instruction Manual

God made men, men made money and money made many men mad.

— Suresh Padmanabhan

Handle Money, rather than letting Money handle You.

Handle Money — It Is Safer than Money Handling You

Rule No.1: Never lose money. Rule No.2: Never forget rule No.1.

— Warren Buffett

Visualize yourself playing around with a safety matchbox. Ignite a matchstick and keep holding the stick till it burns your fingers. Can we blame the matchstick for having burnt your fingers? Can we conclude that matchboxes and matchsticks are intrinsically bad? Should the manufacturer be sued for calling the product 'safety matchsticks?'

Certainly not! The way the matchstick was handled was wrong. Handle it with care and you can cook yourself a hearty meal. One wrong act and you could burn your house down. The matchbox is one of man's best inventions as it has made life extremely comfortable for him. But this does not mean that it is devoid of harmful consequences if handled wrongly.

The same holds true for the knife. The knife that helps a housewife cut vegetables and fruits can be used by a thief to slit her throat. A modified version of a knife proves life-saving when a surgeon uses it to perform complicated surgeries. Therefore, how we handle a particular tool determines its use or misuse.

Like the knife or the matchstick, money too is a tool. One must handle money with care so as to experience abundance and bounty in one's life.

At the same time, if handled carelessly, money can ruin one's life completely.

Take a long intense look at your own life, which includes your home and your bank account. You know you are handling money properly if you have a reasonable bank balance and can at the same time, afford to buy what you desire. On the other hand, if you are struggling to make two ends meet and have debts to repay, it is mishandling of money.

Remember friends, money by itself is harmless. It moves the way you want it to. So, you must use it to its fullest potential.

Unearth the Original Instruction Manual of Money

When I had time I had no money, now I have Money I have no time.

— Suresh Padmanabhan

I often ask myself this question as to why people have so many money problems. What exactly do they fall short of when taking the right actions? Do they err in the handling process?

A simple answer to this is illustrated in this example.

Think about your last visit to the market. Every purchase, whether a cell phone or a television set comes with a bill, a warranty and the most important document – the instruction manual. The instruction manual is an essential document that explains exactly how the particular item operates. By not following the instruction manual, you will not understand the working of the equipment and may probably end up damaging the equipment.

The instruction manual has a very important role in helping the user understand how to operate the gadget. A manual lists various features of the gadget. It also contains a few warnings that you must pay heed to, in order to keep it in good condition.

Isn't money one of man's most amazing creations? Then why don't we have a manual to help us use it effectively? It is the only tool that enables you to enjoy things that give happiness and comfort.

Golmaal: "Your Honour, I want to divorce my wife because she has absolutely no table manners."

Judge: "Well, how long have you been married?"

Golmaal: "About 9 yrs."

Judge: "How come it has taken you so long to understand this?

Golmaal: "Oh! It so happened that I bought a book on etiquette only three days back."

Take the example of a tribal person who does not know what a mobile phone is. If you hand him one, the poor chap will not even know what it is, leave alone how to use it. Without a proper understanding of what it is and how it works, he will not be able to make use of it. But if you acquaint him with the mobile phone and give him an instruction manual, he will slowly and steadily be able to use the mobile phone. It won't be long before he will actually start using it quite well.

Aren't we all using money much the same way as the man unfamiliar with the mobile phone?

Money Bags bought a ten-rupee lottery ticket. To his surprise, he found out the next day that he had won the

Rs 5 million prize money. He rushed to the lottery agent and showed him the ticket. The agent verified the number and found it to be the winning ticket indeed.

Agent: "Please give me some time to pay you the entire amount as the economy is going through a huge recession. Let me pay you a million right now and I promise to pay you the rest within the next two years."

Money Bags: (very angry and upset) "See, for the first time I have won the lottery ticket, I want the complete money now."

Agent: "Ok, if you insist so much, I will try my best to pay half the lottery amount, that is, two and a half million right now. If I don't pay you the rest two and a half million by this year-end, you can strangle me if you wish. This is the maximum I can do for you Sir."

Money Bags: "Get lost. I do not want to fall into this trap. If you cannot give me my 5 million right now, here take this lottery ticket and give my Rs.10 back!"

Most people have no knowledge of how to handle money matters. They are innocent, ignorant and many a time, even stubborn and foolish regarding money matters. Well, isn't it time we discovered the original instructions manual for money?

Report Card of Money

Budget: a mathematical confirmation of your suspicions.

— A.A. Latimer

It is very important to be realistic in our Money World. Realistic means looking at your Money situation as it is. It is the black and white representation of Money. It is a specific number. It is your report card of Money.

Generally we don't tend to look at the Money picture. We have a vague impression of it in our mind. We tend to take a emotional approach rather than an objective assessment of the true picture.

For example: We need to pay our debts. We know we have debts but never look into how much debt we actually have. We keep saying "I have been spending too much money" rather than accounting for the exact amount of Money spent.

It is time to put a number to each of our transactions. Also when we quantify money we are getting a real picture of the current status rather than being in an illusion. So safeguard your money and start taking action.

Let us do a small exercise to know about our money flow. Take a paper and pen and start answering these questions:

1. How much money are you earning per month now?

2. How much was it some years back. Divide the number of years you have been earning into four or five parts. Map it on a graph to show the progress you have made during all your earning phase. If your earnings have dipped any year it will also be revealed. What matters is putting it on paper.

3. How much have you roughly earned all throughout your life. Put an amount alongwith the number of years.

4. How much have you been able to save? Quantify it in terms of savings in bank, fixed deposits, post office etc. This will reveal your savings potential.

5. Do you have any debts if so how much (could be personal borrowings, borrowing from bank etc).

Similarly map out all aspects of Money. Like earnings, spending, saving, investing etc.

The deeper you account in specifics the more clearer picture will be revealed. Now you know specifically the areas of strength and the areas of weakness.

Learn the ultimate language of Money which is being specific and realistic. This way you start gaining money mastery because of the formula, **Measurement = Control.**

Only precise measurement can lead to control and correction. Never fear numbers or the reality they reveal. Even if it is unfavourable you would know how to correct it. This is the first big step of acceptance which will lead your consciousness to plan and handle money wisely.

Action Points:

Start speaking in precise numbers to gain mastery of money;

Write down your present blueprint of money as it is;

Write down your targets in specific numbers along with time frame for fulfilling it;

When you learn to measure money you learn to gain control;

Make it a daily habit. Happy measuring each day.

The Nature of the Instruction Manual

A leaking wallet and a leaking ship both are bound to sink.

— Suresh Padmanabhan

An instruction manual is a handbook meant to give information such as facts on a particular subject.

Isn't there a flaw in the manual if the given instructions are different for different people using the same product? But this holds true in the world of money, the world over. Each one of you goes through life following vague instructions from personal customized user manuals in the head. Furthermore, new instructions are created almost everyday. No wonder one does make blunders in handling money!

You can keep complaining that your money is 'stuck' and feel bad about lack of savings or that nothing is working for you. What you are doing is looking for the right instructions from a faulty user manual. This is much like you calling out to a black cat in a dark room.

A man was sitting under a tree. An apple fell on his head. And the man, Sir Isaac Newton realized there was something beautiful in the phenomenon of things falling down. He went on to discover the laws of motion. My question is, "Didn't the universal law of gravitation exist before its "discovery?" Of course, it did. Just because we were half-asleep when the teacher was explaining gravity does not make the law any less a reality. This applies to money too.

Isn't it time to set things right? Natural laws exist even in the case of money. May be this is a revelation for you at this point. These laws are not very different from the laws of gravity. Both forces are constantly working whether you are aware or not, whether you like them or not and whether you believe in them or not. Your money troubles start only when you begin to impose your own rules which are not in tune with the natural laws of money.

Resolve the conflict between your so-called 'instruction manual' and the 'original instruction manual of money.'

Birth of Your Faulty Instruction Manual of Money

Whoever said health is wealth knew how expensive medical expenses are.

— Suresh Padmanabhan

Leave all things aside and examine your set of rules for money management — your own personal instructions manual. For most of you, the concept of an 'instruction manual' itself is alien. It is as if you have always acted and reacted spontaneously to life. And even if it does exist, it is more or less unstructured and inconsistent.

The faulty instruction manual in our mind has mostly originated from:

1. Wrong inputs in the impressionable years of your life;

2. Faulty conditioning by family and society;

3. Distorted reasoning and wrong conclusions drawn from limited individual experience and lack of exposure to the outside world.

Wrong Inputs in the Impressionable Years of Your Life

Many first loose their health to become wealthy then they loose their wealth to become healthy.

— *Suresh Padmanabhan*

When did your Money Life really begin? You may believe that it was on the day you took your first pay-cheque home. Or perhaps, it was the day your father gave you pocket money.

However the truth is that your money life began even before you were born, that is, in your mother's womb. That was the time when you were most alert and impressionable. You were constantly recording statements, capturing pictures, storing them in your mind's album. It was then that you were most alert and attentive about life.

If your family was poor and depressed, problem areas of money were probably discussed during dinner. That was the time you too started to believe subconsciously, that money was a problem.

At the impressionable stage from minus nine months to the age of seven, the seeds of negativity and false instructions for using money were sown. At that vulnerable age, your power of absorption was high and your ability to reject false attitudes such as money is a necessary evil absent.

Your present thoughts and concepts regarding Money are the result of all the things you have heard and picked up over the years from parents, society, teachers and others.

Thus, depending upon the circumstances unique to your childhood, the seed of a positive or negative outlook on money was sown deep within your subconscious mind and intellect. The way you behave now with money could be a close mirror reflection of the way your parents led their lives. If your father believed that money is scarce then it is very likely for you to have imbibed the scarcity mentality.

It is important to observe and be aware of these influences because at the subconscious level, faulty instructions determine your day-to-day money decisions tremendously. It is also important that you keep a clean and clear mind about this and bear no grudges against anyone (including yourself). The world may or may not be responsible for your problems, but only you have the key to your problems.

You only need to look into your childhood to solve any of your present problems for they all originated there. Let us probe a little more into your childhood.

Reactive Living and Childlike Rebellion

You pestered your parents for a new bicycle. They argued between themselves and also with you. Heated arguments and harsh words followed. Your father stated angrily, "Money does not grow on trees."

You did not get your bicycle that day. You were hurt and you cried. You may have wondered, "Why indeed does money not grow on trees?" It was unfair. "My friend Rahul has one, so why can't I have?" Somewhere deep inside your heart, you resolved to set things right one day. That night you fell asleep crying. It does not matter now whether you got or did not get your bicycle the next day, or next month. Such incidents and your childhood resolutions were imprinted permanently in your mind.

Years later today, you could be leading your life in a rebellious and reactive manner as a spill-over influence from your experiences during your childhood. When you are deprived of anything in your childhood, you will later react in life by either being a big giver or a big depriver.

Remember, however, that there is no need to burden yourself by carrying life-long grudges. Life is an interesting journey and should be enjoyed to the fullest. You ought to have 'reconciled' with such incidents years ago. Learn to give your parents their due for having given so much more. They surely must have had their own compulsions for not having given you the bicycle.

If it still bothers you, you could actually list all the things that your parents did give you. Put it alongside those they did not and could not give. The day you see they are human, just like you, will be the day your relationships with the world will improve.

The bottom line is, when you lead your money life reactively with childish rebellion, always trying to prove a point then you end up totally missing it throughout life.

Faulty Conditioning by Family and Society

A common misconception exists that the spiritual and materialistic paths are different. Actually both originate at one point.

— Suresh Padmanabhan

We inherit not just money, assets and traditions, but also our attitudes of how to deal with money. This legacy is a combination of our genetic make-up and years of classical conditioning by our parents, family and the society at large. Unwritten instructions with flaws miraculously find their way into a faulty instruction manual for money.

Take the example of a person employed in a government office having a man-to-man chat with his grown-up son. He advises the young man to apply for a job with the government, just like himself. However, his son is not interested in doing a 9-to-5 job. He feels his father has wasted an entire lifetime of opportunities by working from 9-to-5 for someone else. He aspires to become a great businessman and set up a shop as a first step towards his goal. The father is shocked. He warns his son against taking up such a risky option. He tries to make him understand that doing business is risky while a government job is safe and secure "Son, this is all what we have done for generations and I'm telling you......... its better that way!"

Little fragments of such mindset lies in all of us. Just like him, many of us want to tread the oft-treaded path when we should really be exploring newer horizons.

The point I'm making here is that we are so conditioned in our beliefs that we tend to believe that the instructions in our personal money manual are the only truth. We thus go through life compromising our actions one after the other. These compromises are between our individual dreams and aspirations and the self-imposed constraints. There is no dearth of people telling you that this is your fate!

Throw away this old and outdated money manual and replace it with a new one, which will work for you. Today, examine your age old money beliefs critically and objectively from root to result! Are they working for you?

Distorted Reasoning and Wrong Conclusions

If spirituality means to include and accept all, then isn't it false for some spiritual people to say Reject Money?

Dr. Jump-to-Conclusion is experimenting with frogs. Frogs have powerful hind legs that enable them to jump well. He is training frogs to jump on command. He ties the right leg tight to the table and commands, Jump! The frog tries to jump with the left leg. He ties the left leg and commands, Jump! The frog tries to jump with the right leg. Now he ties both legs and commands. Nothing happens. Dr. Jump-to-Conclusion therefore concludes that the frog is deaf.

Have you ever been in such a situation in which you draw wrong conclusions from completely unrelated experiences? Quite often our conclusions are a long way off from the truth. There is nothing worse than generalizing conclusions about money.

A friend had borrowed money from you and did not return it on time does not mean, all friends are cheats. You suffered in the stock market, which does not conclude, investing is gambling and so to be avoided. You lost money in network marketing this does not indicate that network marketing is therefore bad for all.

If a person is well dressed, it does not necessarily mean his intentions are as clean as his dress. As they say, appearances are deceptive. At the same time, never underestimate the support you may get from someone you avoided just because you considered him to be illiterate or not well dressed. Even the closest of family members can cheat, while strangers spring from nowhere to rescue you from a problem or a calamity.

Look into your life and check how many money doors you have closed because of your incorrect interpretations. When the doors are closed, how can money come into your life?

I lost heavily in stocks but did not conclude that stock markets are bad. This so-called bad experience helped me understand the markets and today I am happy to see my business successful. I would have closed the door of a revenue stream forever if I had jumped to a conclusion that it was not meant for me.

Don't jump to conclusions or conclusions may jump back at you.

Money Rituals

Money is a completely neutral tool. In the hands of the good, money is fantastic. In the hands of the evil, it can cause great damage.

— Suresh Padmanabhan

You Respect Money and Money Respects You

If money is a source of all your evil. I will gladly accept all your evils.

— Suresh Padmanabhan

The Money Workshop was about to begin. Enrolments were on. A well-dressed gentleman, wearing a designer safari suit, entered the hall. He appeared to be completely engrossed in himself and did not think it worthwhile to wish the courteous receptionist who wished Good Morning, Sir. He pulled out a wad of notes and flung the fees on the table. The receptionist was unnerved and uncertain not knowing how to respond. I took over and requested the gentleman to pick up the money from the table and hand it over with courtesy to the young lady.

He asked, "What is the point? I have paid the money. It is the fees; isn't that enough?" I was adamant. He took some time and then handed the money over to the receptionist. She took it with a smile and a "Thank you, Sir." The man nodded in response. Then he turned to me with a questioning look and asked again, "What is the point?" I assured him that he would surely get his answers during the money workshop.

The Workshop started as scheduled. In the course of the workshop, two participants started sharing their experiences. They had once owned cars, huge houses, and had a lot of money. They had their own company with a number of people working for them. They had been very wealthy at one point in time but all that was in the past. They had now lost all their wealth and affluence. They confessed that when things were going well they had lost their respect for Money. They would literally throw money at people. They handled their money carelessly. And now they had no Money.

During the lunch break, the rude and arrogant man sought me out. He seemed apologetic for his behaviour prior to the session. It was quite clear that he had learnt a very important lesson during the session. After thanking me profusely, he apologized for his rude behaviour in the morning. He had found answers to his questions as to why money ought to be treated with respect scientifically in the Money Workshop. I was happy for him. It is true that man can definitely learn from his own experience in life. But then he can learn a lot more from other people's experiences.

If you want your money to multiply, respect the money you have. Worship it and give it due importance. It is because of this belief, in India a lot of importance has been given to the, **Goddess of Wealth – Lakshmi**.

Organizing Money Is Organizing Life

How can you blame money, a mere tool? Outcomes of both good and evil lie ultimately in your handling.

— Suresh Padmanabhan

Take out your wallet and examine it now. Is it full of visiting cards, bus tickets and old bills? A disorganized wallet is an indication of a disorganized money life and confused thinking.

To begin with corrective action, you must buy yourself a good wallet. You should select one that is sturdy yet attractive. Your wallet is the place of residence and home for your money. Just as it is joy for you to stay in a home that is neat and tidy it is joy for your money to stay there too. In preparing a place for money in your wallet you are preparing yourself for the inflow of excellence into all quarters of your life. Focus on the combination of thought and feeling that money will now come in plenty to stay. Do this right away!

Next, get rid of all the clutter in your old wallet. We often dump those bus tickets, torn visiting cards, scraps of paper with telephone numbers and other paraphernalia in our wallets. Go through each and every bit of paper and then, get rid of all stuff that is of no use to you.

Organize the currency notes in your wallet. Always arrange them in their order of denomination. This also reduces the chances of carelessness while removing money. Besides, it will be easy for you to count and account. Have you seen cashiers in a bank at work? They work calmly and carefully while dealing with money. They give their total attention to the task of accepting or handing out cash.

A disorganized money life is like sleeping in a house full of dust and cobwebs. You can start by eliminating all physical elements of money clutter in your life. Just like gathering up a pack of cards thrown haywire, you too need to gather all the scattered money from around your home in one place. Maybe you have some of your money lying under a pillow or in the kitchen drawer or under the paper in the cupboard, stowed away for a rainy day. Well, it's high time you got it together and arranged it well.

Once this is done, you will automatically extend this habit to other spheres of your own money world. This includes organizing your share certificates, mutual funds certificates, passbooks and other important money-related documents. If you're in a business in which there is regular cash collection, be sure to keep your money systematically and not over-crowded and in an open drawer. Organized money leads to an organized thought process and promotes flow of positive energy.

How Comfortable Are You with Figures Apart from the 36-24-36?

The day you become comfortable with money you also become comfortable with life.

— *Suresh Padmanabhan*

You can test yourself right now. Can you tell exactly how much money you are carrying in your wallet without actually checking it?

Barring a couple of people here and there, I'm sure the rest will not be able to answer this. Take a moment out of your hectic and fast-paced life and do count out the contents of your wallet. Knowing how much money you carry at any given point of time indicates your money consciousness.

If you do not know how much money you carry at a given point, how can you expect to understand the concept of Money in a larger perspective?

If you were in debt, do you think you would be able to write down the exact amount to the tune of a thousand rupees plus or minus? If not, look towards examining why not. Why does thinking about debt alone make you uncomfortable? One derives tremendous power and confidence when one is aware of one's financial status. Besides working consistently at improving one's monetary state of being is what the truly wealthy do. Of course, financial security and stability are not achieved overnight. This process takes desire, planning and creativity. But the most important requirement here is discipline.

Discipline = Freedom = Abundance

Extend this newfound awareness of money to other areas of your life. Money is after all a number game. You ought to know how much savings you have in the bank, how much money you have invested in the stock market, how much money you owe the bank as well as how much is due to you from people you have lent it to.

From now on, make a silent pledge to keep a close track of how much money you carry with you every day.

The Power of Money Consciousness

"The path I advocate is the straight path that says money and deep spirituality can co-exist."

— Suresh Padmanabhan

Name some Money Conscious communities in India.

You can say Marwaris, Gujaratis, Sindhis, Punjabis, and from the south Indian communities Chettiars and Nadars. One also comes across Jews who are highly money conscious.

Money is a very natural effortless process in the minds of those who are money conscious.

I have heard of an interesting story that will demonstrate the power of consciousness:

In an island in Japan there lived a group of monkeys. There was ample growth of sweet potatoes all over the island. Though the monkeys loved the taste of sweet potatoes, they found the muddy murk unpleasant.

One day a cute little monkey grabbed a sweet potato and ran up the tree to devour it. The sweet potato slipped off its hand and fell into a stream of flowing water. The little monkey ran after the sweet potato and grabbed it once again. By then the flowing water had washed off the dirty mud. For the first time possibly the little monkey was having a sweet potato without any mud attached to it. The sweet potato tasted very sweet now. This little monkey had discovered a new process of washing the sweet potato and hence always threw the potato in water before eating it. Slowly the other monkeys also started copying this behavior. Over a period of time the entire group of monkeys on that island was eating washed sweet potatoes a cultural evolution had taken place.

There was an island far away and absolutely unconnected with this island where there were many monkeys and an ample growth of sweet potatoes. It was observed that colonies of monkeys there also started applying the same behavior. Now the amazing question was how did this happen, since there was no access to the island the monkeys were not aware of the existence of their bretheren on the other side.

As the conscious vibrations in this island had reached a critical mass the vibration got picked up by the monkeys in the far away island.

This is the way consciousness travels. This phenomenon applies for anything in this world. When only a limited number of people know of a new way, it may remain the conscious property of only these people. But there is a point (critical point) at which if only one more person tunes in to a new awareness, the field is so strengthened that this awareness is communicated to almost everyone!

When a certain critical number achieves awareness, this new awareness is communicated from mind to mind!

When a large majority in the same community is aware and conscious of money then the community is said to be money conscious. This consciousness becomes natural and is accessible to all.

> Tejas was just a 10 year child coming from a Marwari family. He was so conscious of Money that when he went with his family to a restaurant, he would always cross check the bill before his father could pay. He would be quick to notice any error and point it out immediately. He found out the best offers available for any product or service. He was an encyclopedia of perfect information relating to money. I even observed him correct and reprimand his parents when they made a money mistake. I would be doubly conscious in his presence lest I make a money mistake, as he was sharp and observant.

The interesting thing was that in his presence everybody behaved with great money consciousness. One small 10 year Tejas was spreading money consciousness so easily. The biggest transformations were happening in his family, they now started taking interest in areas of Money which they had been neglecting.

When most members of a family are conscious of money then the family is said to be money conscious. If in a company or an office, the owners and the employees are aware of money then the company is said to be money conscious. If in a country most citizens are conscious of money then the whole country can speed up on its path of prosperity and abundance.

Mahatma Gandhi got Freedom for India with only two words Quit India. The spark that started from him spread far and wide engulfing the subcontinent and the impossible happened. The British quit the country.

Sow the seeds of Money Consciousness deep in your heart. Who knows? You could become the catalyst of transformation.

The Daily Accounting

We at Chrysler borrow money the old-fashioned way. We pay it back.

— Lee Iacocca

Another invaluable practice in the world of money is that of maintaining daily accounts. Daily accounting is simple but very important. You must account for every rupee that comes in and goes out of your life. Account transactions as they happen. Each one of us has just about ten to twelve transactions each day. Keeping the bills organized and in one place will enhance the process.

Beware that your mind right now must be telling you, "Hey, what big difference is it going to make?" or "nobody ever became rich because of writing their accounts," or anything else that will prevent you from writing the accounts.

Would-be Father-in-law: "I will give you Rs. 5 million when you decide to marry my daughter. Tell me what you will give me in return?"

Malamaal: (Very enthusiastically) "I will give you a Receipt."

It may seem boring or a lot of work, but it is essential to keep a daily check on accounts for holistic money growth and for a factual picture of your strengths and weaknesses. Through precise accounting, troublesome money patterns like excessive spending or poor savings can be curbed.

Even if you hate figures by now, it is not too late to start liking them. Although most people aren't very fond of it, daily accounting has in fact, simplified people's lives. As for me, I too did not very much like this cumbersome process. But today, the same cumbersome process has actually simplified my life, enabling me to control my finances perfectly. Remember Daily Accounts is writing accounts daily and not all the account of the week once a week.

When one calculates accounts mentally, it does not have a clear entity. It is still quite a sketchy patch in the mind and is likely to disappear within no time. But when you write down your accounts, you give your finances the much-needed clarity. You are also able to get a bird's eye view of your expenses. This is called chunking (sorting into smaller bits). Now you can see various headings of accounts very clearly — For e.g. Food expenses, travel expenses, communication costs, rent etc. You can exercise control over money only when you have the details. If you realize that the food bills are high then the next month you can cut down.

Many a time, mere realization that food bills are rising will ensure that the expenses are cut down naturally.

I have great respect for my father, who all through his life time maintained his day to day accounts. He never forgot to write the daily accounts even for a single day. This ensured that he never had to face money problem in life.

You may have hundreds of reasons for not writing your Daily Accounts but once you get into a habit you will be more disturbed if you forget or don't write the Daily Account. Well you can ask anyone who is maintaining their personal Daily Accounts. Oh yes, you can surely check this out with my father!

So arm yourself with a small diary, use an organizer or a lap-top and just get started!

Money Contacts — Every Human Being Is a Potential to Money

"Before you speak, listen. Before you write, think. Before you spend, earn. Before you invest, investigate. Before you criticize, wait. Before you pray, forgive. Before you quit, try. Before you retire, save. Before you die, give."

— William A. Ward

How many of you can sincerely say that your friends, relatives and people in your neighbourhood know exactly what you do for a living? Well, there are many who do not, so somewhere this must be resulting in a loss of opportunity for you. In the long run, this could translate into a loss of money for you. The business that should ideally come to you (assuming you offer a great product/service) is probably going to someone else. Right now, they could be buying products and services from your competitors, just because they do not know you could offer them what they want. You ought to divert this flow of money towards yourself.

Many of you shy away from this task, not realizing the loss that you are causing to yourself. Often, a fear of failure prevents you from dealing with them. Do not get misled by this. Your commitment to your business should be absolute. While you spend good money on advertising your products or services in the media, you shy away from revealing what you do, to people close to you and that too, when it costs nothing and promises to be profitable!

You will soon realize that every person you meet can turn out to be your Money Contact. There is always an opportunity waiting for you, a possibility of generating money from every person we meet. To make the most of this opportunity, we ought to be ready with essential details about who we are, what we offer and how good our product or service is.

The key here is to give this information in a very modest and humble manner without sounding high-handed or pompous. People often get repulsed by such an attitude that reflects lack of etiquette.

Let me give you an example. You are reading my book and are therefore a 'money contact' for me. My name is Suresh; I conduct the Money Workshop — the only one of its kind in the world. Join the Money Workshop to discover the ultimate secrets of money. This will enable you to attract and handle money powerfully and perfectly.

You should be able to say these three standard sentences spontaneously to anyone and everyone you meet. It should become as natural as brushing one's teeth. Every time someone comes to know more about your activity, the person becomes a potential client for you. This consequently increases your moneymaking ability. This is as simple as it can get, right?

You then need to work on the standard sentences, slowly

working on their tone and crispness so that they make the person stand up and take notice. Reflect for a few minutes now and construct these sentences as creatively as you can. Leaving behind a visiting card will be an additional advantage to elicit a prompt response.

Now establishing connection with others will become a truly enriching experience.

More Rituals — Money and Beyond

"When I was young I thought that money was the most important thing in life; now that I am old I know that it is."

— Oscar Wilde

1. Take a currency note in your hand and wish it 'Good Morning'. You may find this a little absurd initially, but when we can greet our friends we can surely greet Money, a good friend too.

2. Pick up a currency and kiss it thereby expressing your love for money. Love is by far, the most powerful energy to attracting whatever you want in life.

3. Take a currency note and keep it close to your heart for a few seconds expressing your gratitude. You must thank money and thank the Lord too, for the money that has come into your life.

4. You must also express gratitude for the tools available to you, which help you in attracting money. Facilities like the

phone, computer, machinery, office space etc help you tremendously in delivering quality products and services, don't they?

5. Express gratitude to your wallet, accounts book, cash box, bank passbook or any other tools connected directly to money.

6. Smile at yourself in the mirror and pat yourself when you perform a task well. This enhances your personal powers and makes you more confident and assertive.

7. When giving money, give it with respect.

8. When accepting money, accept it with respect.

9. Always wish happiness for others when giving money to someone.

10. Generally, whenever you purchase things, try and buy them only when you are in a happy state of mind.

11. Respect and value others' money the same way you would respect your own.

Money — Thoughts to Reality

"The only way not to think about money
is to have a great deal of it."

— Edith Wharton

Money Does Grow on Trees.

Money Does Grow on Trees!

"Money frees you from doing things you dislike. Since I dislike doing nearly everything, money is handy."

— Groucho Marx

Here are some commonly-believed thoughts about Money. Mark a tick against every thought you agree with.

Money does not grow on trees.
Money comes only by hard work and struggle.
It's better to have peace of mind than money.
Only a few can be rich.
Only money attracts money.
More money means more problems.
Love for Money is the source of all evil.

Many of you might have placed tick marks against all the above. These are statements that you have heard all through life. They are deeply embedded in our subconscious mind. Let us understand a little more about thoughts.

Whatever you are today is the end result of your thoughts. Thoughts are the basic unit from which life stems just like the air we breathe which sustains life. Your thoughts provide the motivation for action in your life. Every action taken by you is because of a thought in your mind. Even simple actions like drinking water arise from a thought that you are thirsty. Thoughts are the fuel that not only start action but keep you on the 'action track.'

All events small or big are a result of thoughts. These thoughts that originate in your mind have two bases of origin. The first kind originates from within your own 'Self' quite spontaneously. These are the internally-generated thoughts. You could call these your own original thoughts. The other types are those that result from external influence.

A person either accepts or rejects every single thought that comes into his/her mind. Like the gardener who weeds out the unwanted growth in his garden, we too do the same to the thoughts that come to our mind. In this manner, we maintain our mental balance.

When we see a huge tree, we should give a thought to the small seed that was its starting point. I do not know how many of you know that mangoes come from mango trees. I hear many say that mangoes come from the supermarket or fruit vendors. They are right but the origin of mangoes is the mango seed. Mango seeds alone can produce mangoes and papaya seeds alone can produce papayas.

A thought is similar to the seed. Only this time around it is planted in your fertile mind and moves towards shaping your reality. A mango seed can only create a mango tree. Similarly, every thought has a power within itself to create its equivalent in the dimension of reality. It is the same with money. Money grows on money trees in the garden of your mind. When you accept this seed of thought from me please nurture it and let it grow, so that it reaps fruits (money) in abundance.

Unfortunately many of us do not give a thought to our thoughts. Realize the immense power of thoughts and unleash your imagination to make them work wonders for you!

Our Thoughts Create Our World

"The waste of money cures itself, for soon there is no more to waste."

— M.W. Harrison

Does the world appear the same to all of us or is it different for different people? You might say that although it is same, it does appear different to different people. Sometimes, the world appears happy while at other times, it appears sad. What is the mystery behind this phenomenon?

Go a little deeper and you will realize that when you are happy the world also seems happy. When you are depressed and sad the world also appears to be sad and depressed. Yes, each one of us sees the world through our individual perception. Our internal state determines the way the world looks.

The world is a mirror. It mirrors all our internal thoughts. Whatever perception and thoughts we carry within our heart or mind are reflected in the world outside.

When our perspective changes it's image is bound to change too. All the realities that we see in life reflect our inner representation. And this inner representation is created by our thoughts and perceptions. Thus, controlling our thoughts will bring control over our reality.

There was an architect who did the best of work for years. His design and construction were, acknowledged and appreciated the world over. He had worked for many years and things were now getting a little monotonous for him. He was old and tired now and wanted to quit.

He went to his senior and expressed his thoughts.

The senior architect requested him to work on one last design before he quit. "Give it your best, as you always have. After that, you are most welcome to quit." But, the architect was so bored by now that he ended up doing a very shabby job of it. He failed to put his heart and soul into his work like he had always done.

A few months later, the house that he had designed and constructed was ready. The senior architect thanked him and handed him a bunch of keys to the house that he had just finished constructing. "This is a gift for all the efforts you have put into your work with us for all these years" There was nothing more painful for the architect than to stay in a house that he had designed and constructed badly.

You too are the architect of your life. And you live in the world created by your own thoughts. You are the designer and your life is your home. So it is entirely up to you how you design it.

Hard Money or Easy Money — from Thoughts to Realities

"It's good to have money and all things that money can buy, but it's good too, to check up once in a while and make sure that you haven't lost the things that money can't buy."

— George Horace Lorimer

The maxim "Money comes only by hard work and struggle" has two very damaging effects on the lives of those who believe it. Firstly, all the money in their life will come only through hard work and struggle. Second, they subconsciously end up making things a little harder or more difficult for themselves. Worse still, they make things harder for those around them too. They do not enjoy doing easy things because they believe that easy things do not pay off.

Most people believe that one has to work very hard in order to earn money. Naturally, the few people to whom, money comes easily, become the envy of this majority. For the group that believes only in hard work, my advice is to immediately reject this thought. Change your mindset for the better. Work smart, don't work hard. The few people who believe that money can flow easily into their lives actually end up attracting the money towards them. Notice how happy they are with themselves. You ought to start thinking and believing that, "Money can flow easily into my life." When this seed is allowed to germinate and grow in the hopefully fertile bed of your mind wonderful things will happen. Money will indeed flow into your life in full abundance and your life will flourish and prosper.

You might wonder at this point — Do thoughts really play such a critical role in our life? The answer is an emphatic 'YES'. People with infertile or unimaginative minds may think, "I like the thought of being rich, but I will believe Suresh only when the money comes in." Such an attitude will only pull you back and prevent your subconscious from believing positive thoughts. You must think positive, believe it to be true and then work towards your ultimate goal till it is realized.

This cannot be done in a reverse order. It is almost as if you would accept that a dry patch of land can grow ripe mangoes only if you get a ripe mango in your hands even before the saplings are planted.

All things are created twice — first in your mind and then in your reality.

Donkeys too Work Hard

*'Always borrow money from a pessimist,
he doesn't expect to be paid back.'*

— Unknown

Let us define **Hard Work** at the outset.

W-O-R-K is probably the most-hated word in the world, wouldn't you say? There are very few people who really love to work. It is not an abnormal phenomenon at all. Here is something that will give you a quick answer.

Place a tick mark against your most favourite day:

Monday

Tuesday

Wednesday

Thursday

Friday

Saturday

SUNDAY

You've got your answer! SUNDAY is marked the red-letter day in most calendars around the world. Then there are even those that include SATURDAYs to mark weekends. Holidays too are marked in red for them to stand out (and perhaps motivate us to work harder in hope of holidays). Many of us suffer from Monday blues. Why do we feel relaxed as soon as its Friday evening and why do we get the jitters on a Monday morning?

Work has become a self-inflicted curse, an inner turmoil and struggle. Look around and you will realize that man is the only animal that gets worked up about 'working hard'. Even the animal world works hard to satisfy their needs and wants. The Cheetah runs the fastest among animals. But it does so only to catch its prey or in case of escape. Its efforts are utilized optimally and used only as and when required. The effort that it puts in is natural and commensurate with its need.

Work sounds uninteresting, boring, tough or simply difficult when you do not enjoy doing it. When it is natural to your being, when you enjoy creating something and when you find your true self while doing a particular activity, then work becomes the most meditative state that you could be in. It is bliss. Have you ever seen artists, authors or actors complain about their long and difficult hours of work? That is because, they have found their true calling and they are deeply engrossed in it.

On the other hand, work becomes 'work' when it is forced and unpleasant. It is nothing less than carrying a huge heavy sack upon your shoulders. Suppose your boss gives you a job and tells you, "I want this done by evening." The work you had been doing happily with a song in your heart all along suddenly becomes hard-work. You might even picture the boss as a slave-driver. Memories of movies with slaves being chained to oars — the taskmaster with a whip in hand yelling row, row may flash by in your mind.

Sometimes, hard-working people put in a lot of effort unnecessarily. Furthermore, they seek the extra attention and awe of people around them. When they come home they expect full attention from the wife, the children, even the dog. They expect to be admired by the people around them. When ignored they wallow in self-pity.

A day in the life of a hard-working person can be quite difficult as one can see in the following example:

Everyday, when the clock announces time to start for office, our hard working person wipes off the remains of any smile he may have on his face. He picks up his bag or briefcase with important office papers and trudges out with a heavy heart. The poor person mechanically drives to office cursing everyone on the way. He hates every person he sees. More importantly, he hates himself for being in this state. He does not feel any love or affection for the people, he has worked for years together. Neither do they feel any affection for him. He has been working hard for years together but what has he earned? Neither his presence nor absence makes a difference in the lives of the people he has been working with. And he goes through all this only for the sheer compulsion of earning his salary at the end of the month.

He is mystified every month at the injustice of things. He has worked his heart and soul out but his pay is not commensurate with the work he puts in. To add insult to injury, he has never been able understand why some colleagues who hardly work get paid almost as much as him. Nothing about his work life gives him satisfaction. Here is a story of a hard worker with a similar problem!

One day, a colleague noticed the hard worker limping his way around. After a while they sat down for a coffee. While chatting, the hard worker happened to mention some of the personal problems he had faced in the past few days. He spoke about how things were going terribly wrong for him and how God had selected just him to face such situations. Not only had his wife run away with someone else, but his dog had bitten him and he'd suffered a severe loss in the stock market. Moreover, his shoe had also been pinching him for over a month. "My feet have been killing me for a long time. I have a shoe bite from these shoes." The colleague then asked, "Why don't you get yourself a new pair of shoes and throw these old ones away?" The stunning reply was, "What? Get myself a new pair? And deprive myself of the great pleasure and joy I get every time I take them off!"

What do you think is the problem with our hard worker? Actually, nothing is wrong with the person and nothing is wrong with the work. But something is definitely wrong with his attitude towards life.

Isn't it better to rediscover as early as possible an activity close to your heart, mind and soul? When you stumble upon your core competency, you will be full of zest ready to welcome a brand new day. Every evening you will come home bubbling with excitement, full of energy. Work rejuvenates and rebuilds you mentally, physically and emotionally. When you love your work, you do not mind working for free. People have even gone to the extent of paying money to be able to get some work that they would love doing. Work is worship for them, a party all the way!

Welcome Easy Money

"There is no class so pitiably wretched as that which possesses money and nothing else."

— Andrew Carnegie

How does Easy Money sound to you? Most of you may be shocked at the mention of this concept. It may convey connotations of something earned the wrong way or without having worked enough for it. Till now, money seemed to be the hardest thing to earn. How can it start flowing in so easy? Or so, you may think... Unfortunately, the term 'easy money' has always been tinged with negativity. People have always felt something antisocial or even illegal about easy money. Only bank robberies or hefty inheritances could be easy money. And you would picture yourself cooling your heels in prison jails for having earned that kind of money. Believe me, it is nothing like that. Calm yourself down and read on coolly. We are going to redefine the concept of easy money.

Easy Money is money flowing in naturally and smoothly for every task that you do. It is the straight path that lies between you and money. It is the true reward that you get for an assignment that you deliver. It totally justifies the efforts you put in and the quality of work created by you.

Easy money is both, a thought and an attitude. When you are tuned for easy money, you will automatically visualize ease all through your work process — you receive a good business order, you will carry out your transaction well and your customer will also pay you on time. This pattern will follow you every step of your life. For example: Some of us are fortunate inheritors of land and property simply by virtue of the fact that we are born in a particular family. There have been instances when even well-established businesses have been handed over to a few lucky ones. Its about being in the right place at the right time. Easy money, you ask? For heaven's sake, could it get any easier?

When you have a mind block against easy money, you might get exploited. You will be paid much lesser in relation to the task performed. More time will be wasted in every activity of yours. You will also have to do some extra running around and take more efforts to get your payments. Moreover, even inheritance legitimately yours will get blocked without reason.

If money doesn't flow into your life easily and naturally, then something is seriously wrong with the way you live your life. Tune and open up yourself for easy money, for easy is natural and being natural is very easy.

What Creates Our Reality?

"I find four great classes of students: The dumb who stay dumb. The dumb who become wise. The wise who go dumb. The wise who remain wise."

— *Martin H. Fischer*

It is not going to be easy aligning money if you think it is evil and nasty. You have blamed money for years, for your loss of peace, sleep, and friends. Nothing could be farther from the truth. Unfortunately, a larger section of people still believe in the misconception that, if more money came in, one would stand to lose precious things like friends, sleep and finally one's higher self. This fear stops us from aspiring for wealth. We thus end up blocking our own path and restrict the easy flow of money into our lives.

The truth is, money can only enhance and multiply all what we have. In reality, money is a neutral (harmless) tool. It can give us everything from peace of mind, to wonderful friends, to all things bright and beautiful. Acquire money and use it powerfully. And for that to happen, you need to break down the edifice of your old and faulty money paradigms and open yourself to abundance. Drop stupid beliefs like "by becoming rich I will lose all good things of life. Living in poverty is holy..." It is leading life at half mast by consistently denying your potential.

Money + Our Thoughts = Our Reality.

Whatever attribute you add to money will form your reality. If we add hard work to money, hard work will be ours. If we add losing peace of mind to money we will lose peace of mind. If we add tensions and fears to money we will have tension and fear. You can also choose to add umpteen beautiful attributes to money and all will be yours.

There is nothing like wanting money along with wonderful friends, loving family, contentment, peace of mind, and happiness. It is only a matter of visualizing the attribute along with money and it will be all yours!

Money can coexist and blend in with everything divine and beautiful.

The Blank Page

"The illiterate of the 21st century will not be those who cannot read and write, but those who cannot learn, unlearn, and relearn."

— Alvin Toffler

Many of you must have wondered, why the blank page? Surely, it must have been a mistake, probably an oversight. "I wonder how the publisher could have missed this!" Or you thought the blank page happened only in your book? Such thoughts must have surely passed your mind.

What is the Blank Page in reality? In reality, the page is "Blank-Period!" Whatever you write on this page will be your own thoughts and perceptions. Naturally, there would be numerous opinions attached to a simple blank page.

Deep within the layer of thoughts, opinions and whatever else you have added it is a simple blank page. If you start removing external covering matter, almost like peeling layer by layer of an onion, you would most definitely find the blank page. And it has blank pure space.

Similarly, were we to go on peeling off our own concepts and thoughts and whatever labels we have attached to money, we will soon reach the core of our own being and see that it is nothing except money in a pure form. And then you will see and experience the purity, beauty and the radiance of Money. That is the moment you have stumbled upon the deepest secret of Money, which is 'Money is only Money.'

Money and Conditioning

"The world's best book is your passbook."

— *Unknown*

An Insight from the Camel

"With money in your pocket, you are wise and you are handsome and you sing well too."

— Yiddish Proverb

A caravan of people were traveling from village to village through the deserts of Rajasthan. Since it was close to sunset, they decided to pitch their tent before the cold night set in. As the men got busy, tying their camels with a rope, they realized that they were short of just one peg and a rope. They were worried about losing their camel in the night and so decided to go to the village headman to seek a solution.

The village sarpanch was a wise and intelligent man. The travelers approached him with their problem, "Sir, we are here to ask you for a solution to our problem." The headman listened to their problem and said, "Go near the camel and pretend as if you are tying it down."

Although they had their doubts, the travelers did just as they were told. To their surprise, the next morning, the camel was right there. He had not moved an inch, forget about going anywhere. They untied the other camels and tents to move on with their journey. But this one wouldn't move. Fearing something was wrong with him, they went back to the village head.

"Did you untie the camel?" asked the village head. "Sir, we had not tied it in the first place." The headman said, "My dear fellows, that's what you know. The camel still believes that you had tied him. You pretended to tie him, now pretend to untie him!" The travelers went back to the camel and pretended to untie the rope and remove the peg. They were a picture of amazement seeing the camel get up and move on as if nothing had happened at all.

In his own way, the village head had shown the travelers that the rope and peg were just an illusion which the camel thought to be real.

In the same way, all of us are bound by our thoughts, which are actually not real but appear to be so. We are conditioned in that direction and are thus unable to experience complete freedom. If we assume that we are born in a middle class family and therefore will remain middle class all our lives, then the 'middle class' label will tie us up forever and will not allow us to explore further horizons.

If you simply look inward, into your own life, you will see how much you have been conditioned. The realization of being conditioned is the first step towards breaking free from the artificial chains, which are but an illusion.

Break free from all the limitations and conditioning that limit you.

The Ifs and Buts of Life

"Uno sciocco e il suo denaro son presto separati."

— *Italian Proverb*

"A fool and his money are soon parted."

— *English Equivalent*

Humans are a bundle of regrets. Only if I had taken that business opportunity, I would have been making good money today. *If only I had completed my course in management, I would have been earning a fantastic salary today, not to mention the added benefits. But the reality is that I am miserable, looking at machines day in and out. All this is because my parents forced me to get into engineering.*

This is the sad story of so many enterprising people the world over. They may be in different time zones but their mental state couldn't be more alike. The intensity may differ, but the nature of the frustration is just the same.

Are you doing the same? Are you looking back into the past to blame yourself or someone or life itself for your present miserable situation? Believe me, it is nothing more than just a waste of time. If you do feel bad about your situation, the only way to change it is action. Take constructive steps towards changing and improving your present situation rather than grieve over what should or should not have been done.

If you feel someone else has an edge over you because of educational qualifications, do go ahead and acquire such skills. Remember, insecurity that pushes you to improve yourself is positive. Today, there are numerous options for professionals who would like to pursue their studies while working. Part-time classes, weekend classes and even distance learning has made learning more accessible and possible. Give your ambition a direction to express itself and watch your life transform in front of your eyes!

Kill the ifs and buts and give way to the new today. Stop yourself right at the moment you begin to regret something and dwell in the present moment. For sometime, this may need a conscious effort but you will soon notice this becoming a part of your personality. Friends, do not miss the incredible opportunities that life gives you in abundance.

Letting Go of Your Emotional Baggage

Lack of money is the root of all evil.
— George Bernard Shaw

Do you know how monkeys are trapped in Indian forests? Let me show you how letting go can win you your freedom.

Deep in the Indian forests, a hunter brings a small-mouthed pitcher filled with freshly-roasted peanuts. He places it strategically, somewhere near the tree where the monkeys live. The delicious aroma wafts through the air and entices the poor monkeys. They are unaware of the larger scheme of things and innocently come down, hunting for the peanuts. They find the pitcher and one monkey tries his hand at removing the peanuts, but when he tries to withraw it, he is unable to do so without letting go of the peanuts, he is trapped the hunter swipes down and captures it while the smarter ones flee.

Just like the unsuspecting monkey, we have thoughts and concepts which we are unwilling to let go. Each of us has his/her own money story that we have been lugging around like a bag of bricks for a long time. Our past shuts doors to our present and thus becomes our stumbling block. Remember, what we were, is not as important as what we are or what we can become.

We keep repeating traumatic stories and patterns over and over again without recognizing its inherent futility. No one is really interested in listening to tough times because everyone has their own story to tell, isn't it? Self-pity is an endless pit if one falls into it. Stop sitting on its edge and get on to the road of a positive lifestyle. Your bitter baggage is not just heavy but it is simply unnecessary! Most of the times, it actually hampers your progress towards wealth creation.

Destroy the past! Finish it once and for all. Only then can you pave the way for a bright future. Only then can you make room for newer and better possibilities. So, let us firmly resolve to leave the past way behind where it belongs — in the past.

Sometimes the action you take to stop doing the wrong thing is the most important action you take because it allows you to see more clearly the best solution and option available to you.

The only person that can make you feel or believe anything is YOU alone. Remember that, "I am my own sustainer, I am my own destroyer"

Your feelings are a choice just like your entire life is. Get rid of sad memories, sad thoughts and regrets as soon as possible. Write all of them on a piece of paper and tie it to a big gas balloon. Go to your terrace and release the big balloon. You will see all these negative emotions go away forever. Do what you can but don't live in the past, because it won't let you live in the present moment.

Money Excuses or Money?

"I'd say it's been my biggest problem all my life.. it's money. It takes a lot of money to make dreams come true."

— Walt Disney

Many people shirk responsibility vis-à-vis money. Here's a peek into the world of money excuses…

There are galore excuses that the mind can conceive. Let us take one excuse — the 'geographical excuse.' "This particular village, town, city or country offers no money and therefore I cannot earn enough." Here the money problems are in terms of 'kilometres' rather than 'Rs.' The mind does play games by creating illusions. Like they say, the grass is always greener on the other side of the garden. You think the farther you go from where you are, the more you are likely to earn better. Nothing could be farther from the truth! And its not your fault either… You have been fed with a lot of cattle feed from childhood that there is pot of gold at the end of the rainbow! And the rainbow always ends distantly in the next village, town or city.

A famous Hyderabadi saying goes "A Hyderabadi who leaves Hyderabad makes a lot of money. On the other hand a non Hyderabadi who does business in Hyderabad makes a lot of money. Only God knows whether a Hyderabadi in Hyderabad can make money."

There could be other excuses like Time Excuse or Age Excuse. Like, "those days property was so cheap, if only I had money at that time, I would have been a millionaire now." The age excuse is "I am too young to take this money decision now" or "I am too old to start working."

There are a hundred other excuses that we cook on a daily basis. I do not advise any of you to go probing into excuses any more, rather I would like all of you to know and get this Law of Money by heart.

You can make Money or you can make Excuses.

Which of the above choices do you think is the best?

I am confident that all of you will choose Make money. In order to Make Money you ought to stop making excuses. Both of them cannot exist together. When you remove excuses out of your life you will become more M-Powered (Money Powered).

The Broken Window Technique

"There is a very easy way to return from a casino with a small fortune: Go there with a large one."

— Jack Yelton

I don't know about the validity of this story, but it makes interesting reading and learning.

New York City was much infested with crime, small and large. The Mayor of New York wanted the city to be cleansed of the crime and he requested the Police Chief to do something about it. Many a Police Chief took up this challenge and wanted to solve the problem in different ways. Some wanted more police officers to patrol, some wanted more arms and ammunition, and some wanted stricter rules and laws. However these common solutions only treats the symptoms of the problem. It does nothing to address the root cause of crime nor does it lower it. Finally the mayor approached a officer,who was famous for cracking criminal cases using social psychological methods.

The officer studied the problem and then told the Mayor that he had found a workable solution. The Mayor was pleased and asked, "Do you want more guns? Do you want more forces to patrol? Do you want stricter laws? What do you want?"

The police officer just smiled and said, "Sir, all I need is paint."

The solution was so simple but truly amazing. The police officer had observed that all crimes had a very small beginning, just as the mighty rivers originated from small streams. He had observed that the starting point of crime was Graffiti Writing. Everywhere in New York there were graffiti written especially on walls of subways and trains. No one before him had noticed that. He began by just painting all the subways and trains back, spick and span. Every time the train came and had graffiti on it, the officers painted it back. They kept on doing this without fail and the crime graph in New York came down dramatically.

It is interesting to note the psychology behind the solution. Small criminals like graffiti writers if not nipped in the bud, grow to commit bigger crimes. When these small timers noticed that even graffiti was being noticed and rectified, they were scared to commit bigger crimes and the crime rate came down drastically.

This technique is known as the Broken Window Technique.

If in your neighborhood a window is broken by some miscreants, immediately replace the window and then hunt for the culprit. Not attending to the replacement will cause many more windows to be broken and maybe a house will be broken into. Huge ships have sunk with just a single hole.

When you have a small money problem, it is vital to attend to it immediately. If not attended to it can become bigger and bigger. Some daydreamers just pray that problems disappear by themselves. No problem just disappears, but yes, problems can become more complex and grow out of proportion.

Look around now with awareness at your money issues. Do you sense any small issue out of order? It is possible that you are borrowing more than necessary. It could be that your spending is just increasing disproportionately because you are trying to keep up with the Joneses. Maybe you have no savings. Or, you have delayed paying salary to your workers because of lack of money flow. These are all signs and symptoms like the Broken Window for you to sit up and take notice. Rectify them immediately.

Remember even the mighty Titanic sank.

Impossible or I'm Possible

"He who wants a rose must respect the thorn."

— Persian Proverb

A friend of mine is slightly on the plumper side. He is often unable to walk more than a few metres at one go. He has to rest a few minutes every few steps. I told him once that he could run the fastest if it was a matter of survival. Of course, he refused to believe me.

One April morning, we happened to be taking a stroll when all of a sudden, he started running. I didn't realize what happened so I too ran after him. I could have never imagined him to run as fast as he ran that day. Within minutes he covered nearly a hundred metres. I caught up with him, a long while later. I was gasping and wondering where in heavens he got such strength and speed. He stopped, looked behind and pointed "Did you notice the three mad dogs after us?"

I was amazed at his strong survival instinct. I pondered over the the inherent powers that every living beings possess.

Metabolism of the human body is triggered for activity with chemicals, enzymes and adrenalin being produced to respond to this rather desperate situation. We all know about these capabilities, but hardly bother to push ourselves to seek our true self. We may not realize this now, but these very qualities in us will stand us in good stead in the long run.

If you had someone telling you at gunpoint, "You are going to get killed right now if you don't improve your profitability or increase your turnover by 35%." I'm sure you will work day and night but ensure that you achieve both targets. That is because you value 'life' more than anything else. The question is why to wait for someone to point a gun in the first place? If you can imagine or create a similar situation hypothetically, it will still have the same effect or result. Then you would realize your own potential. You will change the result with a simple change in your attitude towards the same thing. This change of attitude or technique awakens the giant asleep in your subconscious mind.

Money

and

Behaviour

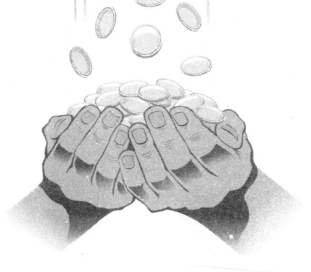

"Don't stay in bed, unless you can make money in bed."

— George Burns

Are You a Carrot, an Egg or a Coffee Bean?

"Our incomes are like our shoes: if too small, they hurt and pinch us; but if too large, they cause us to stumble and trip."

— John Locke

A young woman went to her mother and told her about her life and how things were so difficult for her. She did not know how she was going to make it and wanted to give up. She was tired of fighting and struggling. It seemed as if one problem would get solved only to give way to another one. "Come into the kitchen, dear" said her mother. She filled three pots with water. In the first, she placed carrots, in the second she placed eggs and the last she placed ground coffee beans. She let them settle and kept them to boil without saying a word.

After about twenty minutes, she turned off the burners. She fished the carrots out and placed them in a bowl. She took the eggs out and placed them in a bowl. Then she ladled the ground coffee beans into a bowl. Turning to her daughter, she asked, "Tell me what you see?"

"Carrots, eggs, and coffee," she replied.

She called her daughter closer and asked her to feel all the items individually. The carrots were soft and pulpy, the eggs had turned hard while the coffee beans had turned the water into coffee. But, the coffee spread its rich aroma throughout the room. The daughter realized that her mother wanted to explain to her how one ought to react in adverse times.

So are you a carrot, an egg or a coffee bean?

ASK YOURSELF: WHAT AM I?

Am I the carrot that seems strong, but becomes wilted and soft in tough times? Am I the egg that starts with a malleable heart, but changes with the heat? Did I have a fluid spirit, but after experiencing a calamity like death, a break-up, a financial hardship or some other trial, have I become hardened and stiff? Does my shell look the same, but on the inside am I bitter and tough with a stiff spirit and a hardened heart? Or am I like the coffee bean? The bean actually changes the hot water, the very circumstances that bring on the pain. As the water temperature increases, the coffee beans release more fragrance and flavour. If you are like the coffee bean, you get better when things are at their worst!

Success in life finally depends on how you feel about yourself.

The Big Escape —
Fight or Flight

"It is an unfortunate human failing that a full pocketbook often groans more loudly than an empty stomach."

— *Franklin Delano Roosevelt*

When you encounter money issues, it will either be fight or flight. More often, the mind chooses flight because it is easier than fight. All our responses are conditioned by anticipated pain or pleasure. It is a general rule that the mind likes to enjoy pleasure and avoid pain. We all know that facing a situation, fighting it will invariably cause pain. Running away seems easier and will appear to be a good choice. So, it is no surprise that you may choose to run away from the problem. That is why, when we encounter difficulties, our mind builds a parallel escape mechanism to avoid the pain caused.

Of course, this response varies from person to person. Someone might prefer to isolate himself, to sleep it off or to pretend to be busy. Some others try to meditate, to listen to spiritual talks or to get involved in a creative activity which could help him or her deal with the stress. The mind, on most occasions, will try its best to avoid facing a monetary problem. So every time a problem crops up, your mind will create the same escape patterns.

Most people who want to avoid facing reality behave in this way. Yes, reality is in its truest sense, ugly, painful and uncomfortable. When one wants to escape reality, the mind creates an illusionary state, which makes the person feel comfortable in the midst of undesirable circumstances. Although one does know that this is not really the right response or solution, one is helpless. The subconscious mind triumphs over the conscious mind and you somehow cope up with the circumstances.

You must have realized by now that escapism is not the answer to dealing with difficult situations. One must try to avoid this option by coming up with a more constructive solution.

To be able to do this, you have to discover your individual escape mechanism. If you introspect a little, you will observe that following the escape method leads you to a temporary respite from the problem. It neither solves the problem, nor does it take you away from the problem permanently. Like the cat who laps up the milk with its eyes closed, thinking no one is watching her, you too live a life of make belief thinking and believing that the problem does not exist simply because you choose not to face it. Unfortunately, that is not the case!

Do you want to nip the problem in the bud? Here is a solution:

Recognize your specific escape mechanism whenever a difficult situation arises and try to break it. For example, you may be isolating yourself whenever you are stressed out due to work pressures. Recognize this and consciously try to go out, meet up with friends and socialize a bit. Your mind may resist at first, but you will soon see the stress being eliminated from your life. You need to give your mind newer responses to certain stimuli. Deep down in your mind the structure of avoidance will be shattered. Ensure that you never create such a structure again. And you will be able to face the same problems easily and confidently. Soon enough, you will be on your way to happiness and confidence even in difficult times.

The Law of 100% Responsibility

'Capital isn't scarce; vision is.'

— Sam Walton

Friend to Golmaal: "Should I get married?"

Golmaal: "Yes, you should marry. And my advice is everybody should get married."

Friend: "Why do you say that?"

Golmaal: "Because you can't keep blaming only the Government when things go wrong."

We love to take responsibility of things that are already going great. When things are going well, everyone likes to be held responsible and showered with praise for the success. But if they go wrong, the mind immediately looks out for someone else or something else to be blamed. There are people who blame their past life and the planetary positions if anything goes wrong in their lives.

The human mind brings up two clear lists. The first has the heading, I want this to happen and the other is titled, I don't want this to happen ever! People go through life, reacting to every event against this list. Naturally, they are very happy if they want it to happen and not so happy if they don't.

In the case of events that are not desirable, the mind gets disturbed and the blame game starts. People move from the disturbed state to the very disturbed state within no time. It is only when things go to a serious level that professional psychological or psychiatric help is sought.

If you scratch the surface of most problems, the glaring truth stands out that, others may be responsible for the problem but you, yourself are responsible for the solution. Accept the onus of responsibility for your role in the game of life and get back your personal powers.

Mahatma Gandhi, the father of our nation is one such example of a frail thin man who changed the course of life simply by accepting responsibility. His books and teachings provide an enormous wealth of great spirituality and self-development techniques.

Super Formula – Take Responsibility = Seize Power

You accept more responsibility, you receive more power.

Are You the Candle?

"Never confuse the size of your paycheck with the size of your talent."

— *Marlon Brando*

Look at a burning candle for a while. What do you see happening? As it spreads light, it burns and melts its own self. Yes, it gives light but at the cost of its own death. There comes a time when the candle is unable to do so and soon dies out. Another noticeable thing about the candle is that there is always darkness at its own base although it spreads light far and wide. Are you like the candle?

In the world of money, being like the candle is a serious flaw. If you have helped others, shed light in their homes, and never was there any reason to complain then it is okay. I have nothing to say. But if you have put your own needs last and paid little or no attention to your own needs, you have been unfair to yourself. Have you unnecessarily supported other people even at the cost of your own detriment? You haven't done the right thing.

Picture this. A man is drowning. He screams for help. You jump to help him. There is just one small hitch — you can't swim. Now there are two men screaming for help!

Remember, any help or support you extend should always come out of a position of strength. If you have a piece of bread, give half of it, not the entire piece. Think of what will happen to the millions of people starving the world over if kind-hearted people like you perish due to starvation?

Do not end up becoming the sacrificial lamb. The next time you reach out to someone ensure that you do not sacrifice yourself in the process.

There once lived a donkey and a bull in a vast field. The bull was tired due to the repetitive nature of his task. He approached his friend, the donkey to seek his advice on what to do to get out of the backbreaking work. The donkey felt bad for his friend and advised him to pretend being sick. The next day when the farmer came to drag him to the fields he saw that the bull was not well. The bull did a great job of acting sick and much as the farmer tried he just did not budge. The farmer got very upset that morning. He caught hold of the donkey, put the yoke on him and made him do the work that the bull was supposed to do. The task was not the donkey's cup of tea and he had to struggle with it long and hard. The poor donkey kept working the whole day under the hot sun, while the bull rested comfortably in the cool shade. The bull, capitalizing on the donkey's willing stupidity, trapped the donkey in a vicious cycle of hard work by feigning illness whenever he wanted to get out of work. By the end of the month, the poor donkey's back was almost broken.

If you're like the donkey, if you are doing other people's work, are busy being charitable when you're the one in dire need of charity, when you are always putting others' needs before your own and suffering for it in the bargain. Maybe you need to give yourself over to some serious introspection. You are not doing anybody any good. The story of the farmer, donkey and bull does not end there. The farmer then decided that it was no use keeping a sick bull. He sent it away and bought a new one.

Do not become a sacrificial lamb in this world. Work hard and earn what is rightfully yours.

Are You the Doormat?

Life shouldn't be printed on dollar bills.

— Clifford Odets

Have you noticed a doormat carefully? It lies there at the entrance, only to be trampled upon by one and all. People wipe the dirt off their feet on it for years. And years later, bruised, torn and ripped apart, the doormat is flung away without a thought. A new one replaces it almost immediately. Have you ever heard a doormat protest?

Are you behaving like a doormat? Do people trample over you to get ahead while you stay exactly where you are? Are you being used as a stepping stone for other people's success? Do people extract work from you without paying your dues? And do you remain silent without even a slight protest?

Such behaviour is carried over from your childhood, where you always did things to get that good boy or good girl pat on your back. Okay, you have got yourself a good guy image but you have also got yourself the go for image. Go for this and go for that. You are sent on errands by all and sundry. And your life has now become no different from that of a doormat.

Stop behaving like a doormat from now. Watch out as this pattern becomes repetitive in whatever you do. When the remote control of your life is in somebody else's hands, it is but natural they will start pushing the buttons and you get manipulated.

Once there lived a big and powerful cobra in the jungle. He terrorized people who entered the forest. One day a holy man came into the forest. He did not fear the cobra at all. He decided to teach a lesson to the fiery cobra. Just as it was about to strike at him, he caught it. Looking straight into the reptile's eyes he said, "You better change your ways. Why are you trying to bite everyone?"

Since that day the cobra changed its ways. It became docile and just lay down at one place. People who ventured into the forest were scared when they saw the cobra, and pelted stones at it and beat it up with sticks. The cobra was helpless and lay half-dead. The holy man happened to pass by. His heart went out to the cobra. He asked him sympathetically, "What happened to you?" The cobra explained that he had obediently followed his advice. He had stopped biting people or scaring them. The holy man then said compassionately, "You poor fool! I had only asked you to stop biting. But then why didn't you hiss at least? Don't you know how to protect yourself?"

A doormat has no voice and makes no protest, but I bet you can. Why don't you, for a small experiment, just kick yourself once and yell naturally? Now you are prepared to yell and assert your God given rights.

Power of NO

"I'd like to live as a poor man with lots of money."

— *Pablo Picasso*

Most of our money issues arise because we are unable to assert ourselves to come up with a simple NO. Let us say a friend comes to you to borrow money. Deep down you want to say NO but you are not able to refuse. You need the money yet you sacrifice and give it to him; maybe its even money borrowed from others. Later you wallow in a puddle of your own remorseful tears.

Many of us grow up as people pleasers. We feel if we say NO the other person might feel offended. There is also a fear that we might lose a friend if we do not give in to a request. What we do not realize is that it is very important to say a polite yet firm NO at appropriate times. You should not let people get away with manipulations because of our inability to say NO.

Often, saying NO is difficult because of the foolishly-imagined consequences.

Mr Never-say-No: "People keep borrowing money from me and they never return it." (sob sob sniff sniff.)

Money Bags: "Why do you lend them money then?"

Mr. Never-say-No: "I'll lose friends if I don't. They will think I'm a mean person."

Here, the imagined consequence is of losing a friend because of saying NO. If your friendship is so flimsy that it can break on just saying a NO then it is better that it breaks. You part away with money to protect all this. And money gets stuck. Now, ironically, not only you have lost friendship but also your money.

When we think too much about the consequences, then saying NO becomes difficult. Hence say NO and then think. Remember that NO is the most powerful word in the money dictionary. The world's top leaders say NO more number of times than saying YES.

There are four stages of saying NO. First is the stage where you just cannot say NO. Second is the Stage where you say NO and feel guilty. Third is where you say NO and justify. The last is a plain and straight assertive NO. The earlier you evolve and reach the fourth stage the better it is going to be for you.

Now you are ready for the consequences. If you still find it tough, you can convert it into a fun game. Practice different ways of saying NO till you can say it effortlessly. You may choose to say NO blindly wherever it is required for the next seven days. At the end of seven days you will have mastered the power within you. You will be surprised to see the world take notice of you once you are able to achieve this amazing skill.

How Do We Get Manipulated?

'All I ask is the chance to prove that money can't make me happy.'

— Spike Milligan

No one likes a person who is in control of himself. People like to dominate over others, manipulate others and generally get their way around. So let me make you aware that when you start using the principle of saying NO, people are not going to react well to you, at least initially. They will wonder where your vulnerable and gullible personality has vanished and they will naturally take a little while in adjusting to the new improved you.

So naturally, people will look for all possible ways to manipulate you. Read on....

The weapons of manipulation that you need to watch out follows: Good certificates: A 'friend' asks for a loan of ten thousand rupees. You exercise your newfound power and say 'NO'. He then starts to manipulate you by giving you a good certificate. He starts to extol your virtue and whines, "You're the only one I know with a charitable heart."

If you do give him the ten thousand rupees that you did not want to give, you have traded the money for a good certificate from him. But if you persist in refusing, he will realize that the good certificate gimmick has not worked. He could then try another approach, the bad certificate gimmick. He may then subtly say, "Okay! That does not matter. I think I'll go ask our common friend Mr. X." Beware! This is actually leading you to believe that common friends will be shocked when they know how mean you can be that you could not afford to give this small loan. These bad certificates are given to make you feel guilty.

If you succumb to these pressures and give the money, you might feel good having escaped the guilt trap. But, the reality is that you have been manipulating into trading your money for the dubious advantage and comfort of not getting a bad name.

Please don't succumb to the lure of a good certificate or the stigma of a bad one because, either way, you will be prone to lose money. My life became powerful when I stopped accepting good or bad certificates from the market. Now I had stumbled upon my own power centre and therefore could not be manipulated. I had discovered the advantages of knowing myself and feeling good about myself. I still accepted the good certificates as a bonus but the certificates never influenced my decisions.

Throw the certificates out of your life and allow your own powers to rise above all this.

Crib and You Will Have More Real Situations to Crib

I'm so naive about finances. Once when my mother mentioned an amount and I realized I didn't understand. She had to explain: 'That's like three Mercedes.' Then I understood."

— Brooke Shields

I remember my friend's mother who used to perpetually complain. She'd complained more when she encountered bad incidents. She invariably complained for all money matters.

She had a peculiar habit. Whenever she had to spend money, she would feel very bad. She would complain at the electricity bill and blame that the electricity board was cheating her. She would complain and blame the telecommunication company for sending her inflated bills. She would complain when her children asked money for their college. Her life was full of complaints.

Over the years I have been observing her, and I noticed complaining had become her second nature. Soon there was a downturn in her life and she faced genuine financial problem. All the money she had saved was lost in wrong investments. The precious jewellery that she had bought for her daughter's marriage was stolen. Her son fell sick and she had to spend on hospitalization. She lost much more than she gained in life.

Be warned that always complaining is an energy block. The more you complain about money the more money runs away from you.

Complacency Is the Biggest Stumbling Block to Money

"Someone stole all my credit cards, but I won't be reporting it. The thief spends less than my wife."

— *Henny Youngman*

What happens when you lose money?

Let us assume you lost Rs. 2 lakhs; you initially feel bad about this. Now you want the whole world to know about your loss. You meet a good old friend one day on the streets and he makes the mistake of asking, "How are you?" This is enough for you to unburden your sob story of the loss. As he hears you patiently, you sense that his cheerful face is turning sad. Your loss has triggered an incident from his past. He remembers that he too had lost a lot of money many years ago. And he is really feeling bad about being reminded of the loss. But something interesting is happening to you. Deep down you already are feeling better. In comparison you have only lost Rs. 2 lakhs while he has lost Rs. 5 lakhs.

You are touched and want to help him out. So both of you go

all the way to meet another friend of yours and share your story of the loss. It turns out that this friend has lost over Rs. 10 lakhs in the stock market. He is terribly upset of being reminded of this huge loss. When you look at the face of the friend who lost Rs. 5 lakhs, he is already feeling better, for his loss is much less. And you are feeling exhilarated already. What is Rs. 2 lakhs now in comparison with Rs. 10 lakhs? You can always find someone who has lost more money. Now you are like the scientist who has discovered a new money formula.

It is alright to lose money because everybody is losing it someway or the other. This way, all through life, we keep tolerating any loss. We become thick-skinned, immune and complacent. But remember, sometime in life you might have earned about Rs. 5000 per month. It takes 12 months to earn Rs. 60000. It takes 10 years to accumulate Rs. 6 lacs. You lose much more money in a matter of days and if it doesn't even pinch you to take action, it is sheer complacency.

Do understand, it takes every single drop to build the huge reservoir that supplies gurgling water to thousands of people. It takes every single rupee to build a fortune. Every money loss, small or big, matters. This should pinch you awake from your deep slumber and enable you to take a corrective action.

Is Your Money Built on a Foundation of Sacrifice?

"If you think nobody cares if you're alive, try missing a couple of loan repayments."

— Earl Wilson

A few days ago, my friend's uncle dropped in for a chat. He is a nice down-to-earth and honest gentleman — retired government official. After some trivial chatter, our conversation veered towards the subject of financial management. I asked him how much money he'd managed to put away over the last few years. His answer left me dumbfounded. He was worth half a crore. This man of moderate means had managed to put away a tidy sum of 25 lakhs in asset creation and 25 lakhs of savings in hard cash.

I got curious. When people's savings are so bad, here was a master saver. I wanted to get down to unraveling the mystery behind his huge savings.

He confided after much coaxing that all his life he had never learned to spend. Dining out was taboo. On the rare occasion that he did dine out, he ensured that it was the other person footing the bill. New clothes were an unheard extravagance. The only marriage ceremony he was likely to attend was one where there was a possibility of him getting a gift of new clothes from either side. When he had to make certain mandatory trips out of station, he never bought the local curios he loved nor did he do any sight-seeing. He did not get married and truly believed that it was the smartest money-saving move he could have made.

Here was a man who was rich technically on paper. But, according to me, he was a very poor man, since, short of wearing rags, he had spent his entire life living like a pauper. He had robbed himself every moment to create this wealth. At 65 years of age, retired, he had nobody whom he could call his own. He had no wife, no children who could inherit this wealth. All his life he knew how to make money. However, the other dimensions of money had been cut off, making him very imbalanced.

I took pity and suggested that it might be a good idea to spend some money on himself for a change. At this point, he screamed murder and confided that he was looking for ways to make his half a crore into a crore. I felt a pang of sorrow for this poor little rich man standing in front of me.

Months later, I heard that this same gentleman died a very miserable death. He was diagnosed with cancer and died a painful death in a local hospital. No one was at his bed side to support him during his last days. I last heard that his half a crore is still under litigation and his relatives are fighting a bitter battle in the court to get the money.

In light of this story, pause for a moment and ask yourself what epitaph you would like to see etched on your tombstone.

Whatever it is...I hope it does not read as.......

Here lies..................... (Your name goes here)

Made lots of money

Did not spend any

Now dead, is this funny?

When Death Gives You a Report Card of Life

"My problem lies with reconciling my gross habits with my net income."

— Errol Flynn

This could be a useful exercise: picture yourself dead and imagine what your relatives and friends are saying about you. Are they happy that you are gone for good? Are they accusing you of having created wealth at their expense and are glad that you cannot use it, now that you are no longer alive? Or are they grieving at the loss of a dear person whom they valued deeply?

In death, the most truthful evaluation will come across — one that can shock or numb you. Because while you are alive, and especially in a powerful position, no one dares to give you the right feedback. Who would like to invite your wrath? And all your life you keep thinking that people around you meant when they said you were a nice person. People don't say what they mean and at times don't mean what they say.

All your life you lived in an illusion because of the false assessment.

It is important to know yourself because the best critic and analyzer is your own conscience. It does not matter whether the world gives you a great character certificate or terms you a terrible person as long as you know what you are.

So while you are alive introspect deep within yourself. Look at your actions. Are they hurting anyone? Is your life standing on people's curses or resting beautifully on their blessings and good wishes? Be honest and evaluate your attitudes in the money world.

Are you a person who is using his/her money to uplift those around you? If so, you are surely a very noble person and a responsible member of society. The countless blessings that you will get from the people whose lives you touch will hold you in good stead. On the other hand, if you are using your money power to dominate over others and exploit them, you are not just eroding the society but are also doing yourself great damage by inviting the silent curses of those people who are suffering your atrocities.?

If somewhere you feel that you are wrong then transform yourself from within. Your conscience is the most priced possession you have. You can cheat the whole world but never yourself. When you look into the mirror, you shall see the truth always, not what you want to see. If you are a straightforward, kind and honest person, you shall see the glow of such a person in your face. If not, you will find it difficult to look at yourself in the eyes. As they say, life is short, enjoy while it lasts. I would go one step further and say, life is short, do the best you can for others so that you live long after you are gone. Live the truth and then truth shall set you free. You live only once so why not live respectably.

Don't wait for Death to give you a report card of your life.

Has Your Photograph Appeared in the Obituary Column?

They who are of the opinion that Money will do everything, may very well be suspected to do everything for Money.

— George Savile

As you read this you might be more dead than alive. Do I sound crazy or rude? Please read on.

Money Bags was born in the year 1955. He died in the year 1975 and was finally buried in the year 2001.

Now, before you label me as insane, let me relate his story to you. Money Bags lived joyfully only the first twenty years of his life. The rest of the years, he was as good as dead. He led a mechanical existence.

Look around and you will see many dead people walking — People devoid of curiosity, aliveness and zest that characterized their life of yesteryears are simply bored now. How can a living person be bored with life? The English language has words such as zombie and even the phrase half-dead. Either you are dead or you are not dead. There is no mid-way in the journey of life.

So, tomorrow when you get your newspaper, check the obituary column to see if your photograph is in there. If it is, then all your problems are solved! You are truly and officially dead! If not, it is an indication that you are alive. Then, please live life King Size or Queen Size, with renewed passion, verve and elation. Justify the life that you live. From this moment on, ask yourself at every phase of the day. **Are my actions Alive or Dead?**

God was seated on his throne in Heaven and was thoroughly bored. He was playing around with his magic wand. He decided to have some fun and created the donkey. He gave him eighty years to live. The donkey whined pitifully "Oh! Good Sir. I just want to live for fifty years." And God in all his magnanimity said, "So be it."

Then God rested for a while before creating the dog. He gave him sixty years to live. The dog pleaded that it be given only forty years instead of sixty. God said, "So be it."

Then the monkey was created. God gave the monkey sixty years to live. The monkey wept, "Oh! God in your mercy and wisdom give me forty years, not sixty." And so, the monkey had a life span of only sixty.

And finally God created the human being. He granted him only twenty years. The human being got very upset with God for giving the donkey, dog and monkey more years than him. He was fine with his 20 years and requested God to give him the 30 years of the donkey, 20 years of the dog and 20 years of the monkey, which they had refused.

God said, "So be it!" and sent the human being to earth.

After that, the human being lived for 20 years with the qualities of the human being. The next thirty years he worked hard, just the way the donkey did and carried the burden of money worries. During the subsequent twenty years, he kept guarding his wealth like the dog. Last twenty years he spends like a monkey jumping from one son to the other, to be taken care of in his old age.

I invite you to live like a human being.

Money — Personal Powers

The safe way to double your money is to fold it over once and put it in your pocket.

— Frank Hubbard

Survival of the Toughest

Only when the last tree has died and the last river been poisoned and the last fish been caught will we realise we cannot eat money.

— Cree Indian Proverb

I once got caught up in a traffic jam. I got out of my car to see why the cars wouldn't move. The reason was big, fat and black – a buffalo! It sat right there in the middle of the road, coolly chewing cud in the same manner we chew gum. Completely oblivious to the din of the cars and completely indifferent to the trouble it was causing everyone around. It was totally indifferent to all the honking and cajoling. Its owner tried everything possible to get it to the side of the road but all his efforts were in vain. The harrowed motorists were also trying to somehow get ahead.

Of course, the buffalo got up after a while and walked away as if nothing had happened in the first place. Some one from the crowd there said at that moment, "that's surely a thick-skinned animal."

You need to learn the art of striking out on your own. The world is tough and also there are characters constantly nagging at you. While in the jungle no animal dares to attack the tiger or the lion. The deer and the rabbits are always preyed upon. The weak are vulnerable everywhere.

In the jungle of our money world only the toughest can survive.

Power of Being I-centric

Give me a million dollar and I will spend all of it in just a day say many. But few would dare to say, "give me a million dollar and I will make it a billion."

— *Suresh Padmanabhan*

There are billions of people in the world but not one is as unique as you. There is only ONE you. God has created you as an individual — even finger prints don't match. Thus all of us have our own personal powers. So, all money issues too are so individual in nature. Therefore why should one behave with a herd mentality?

If you take a half-filled glass and keep pouring water into it, you will soon see a spill-over after the glass is completely filled. Similarly you too can give to the world only what you have. If you have knowledge overflowing from you, the world will receive it, if you have money overflowing from you (but in the right direction), the world will benefit from it and so on. This is called the power of being 'I-centric' where everything originates out of your centre.

I-centric is not being selfish. It is helping out people where needed but from a powerful state. Fill up the 'I' with what you want to give to the world — be it money, love, gratitude, charity...

I-centric is also protecting your individuality and your powers, for there are enough people around you who steal it — knowingly or unknowingly. Let me give you a day-to-day example:

I used to travel in an auto rickshaw in Chennai. The Chennai auto guys are notorious for rounding off to the next highest denomination of the meter. So if the meter shows Rs. 22/- then they would calculate it as Rs. 30/- Many would let go the remaining change to avoid arguing with them especially since they were very rowdy and foul-mouthed. After paying the auto fare I used to wait patiently for the change, this annoyed the auto drivers. In order to justify their reasons behind keeping the excess change some would say "Sir, you carry a mobile phone, you look decent, then can you not leave the change for a poor hard-working man?" To which I smilingly reply, thanks to small savings like this, a hard working person like me is able to buy a mobile.

I was guilt-free because I paid them their due and only fought for my rightful money to come back to me.

The question here is not the small change, but your own personal powers. If an auto driver can get away with this, then imagine how much of your individuality and personal powers you must be losing on a regular basis. The danger is this builds a repetitive pattern and you will start attracting more such persons in your life who will steal your powers. So always fight for your right and protect your personal powers.

Examine closely the safety instructions given in planes for

starters. 'In the event of an emergency, oxygen masks will descend from the overhead compartment... please secure your own mask before assisting your child.' The rationale behind this instruction is the same all over the world. A calm and composed parent is better equipped to comfort a frightened child the same way only someone completely secure in the money world is capable of handling money well. When you are perfect you can assist others to be perfect.

I-centric means taking money decisions from your own self rather than from others. For instance, do you find yourself coveting a new big car just because your neighbour has one or do you want desperately go to New Zealand just because your great aunt's step-son's mother-in-law says it is a must-see location? And do you also want a penthouse, after all what will your friends think otherwise, right? If the world invests in stocks, should you? Without stopping to reflect or ponder whether you really know all about stock markets. This is known as herd mentality — doing what others do.

If you go out of your way to satisfy the world, chances are that you'll never end up satisfying anybody, least of all yourself. For a change, look at what you need instead.

The day you start taking money decisions based on self-interest you awake to the joys of intrinsic satisfaction. Wouldn't it be much nicer if you bought that new car because you thought you deserved it, or you invested in the stock market because you want to make money and not to please Mrs. so and so, who doesn't give a damn anyway?

Pat yourself on the back when you succeed in living up to the demands of the I-centric new you. There's sure to be a spring in your step and a twinkle in your eye as you rediscover the power of your own individuality.

Power of Receiving

Money is neither my god nor my devil. It is a form of energy that tends to make us more of who we already are, whether it's greedy or loving.

— Dan Millman

Just about everyone you have met and heard has spoken about the importance of giving. It has been your staple diet since you had your first set of pearly white milk teeth. You may even have convinced yourself that you will be blessed more when you give.

It is time that you now hear about receiving. All those who taught you to give became receivers. You will have proof of this when you remember all those to whom you have given Money. You have been brainwashed with benefits here and/or the hereafter when you give. To ensure that there were enough givers well conceived social and mass propaganda systems were developed, and the mass kept on giving.

It is important in the above system that there are fewer

receivers than givers. To be sustainable the system requires more givers and less receivers. Otherwise the share per receiver becomes less and the system becomes unstable. So, thinking was also influenced to make people believe that to receive was basically demeaning. Look at your own self closely. Can you see how well all that brainwashing has worked? Don't you feel great when it comes to giving? And is there not discomfort when you have to receive.

Everything that you have wanted has to come to you through the doorways of receiving. Your wants may be new business opportunity, love, happiness, customers and money too. You have conditioned your mind and put a mental block against receiving. It is like inviting someone, locking your doors from inside and then wondering why you are without company. As we go away from our natural state to receive we experience great inner struggle. This is the single biggest block for money flow in your life.

When you go to purchase a mobile phone, don't you check its receiving powers? You need to apply the same principle in your own life and check your receiving power. You might be scared at times when you receive. A thought going in most minds is, "What if people give me things and then pester me for favours that I do not like to do." And in the process you miss out receiving altogether. Receive graciously and thankfully as long as you're not compromising on your morals and values. Under no circumstance should you lock yourself in for hypothetical fear. Remember faith and fear cannot stay together in one place.

The receiving is not about some mundane alms or charity. Out there in the open world, each and every plant opens out its being to receive the bounties of nature, sunlight, nutrients and minerals. This ultimately has sustained the different forms of life on this planet for countless years and will continue to do so for many more years to come.

All forms of life and existence are always in the receiving state. Have you got any doubts? Check this out with your friendly neighbourhood spiritual Guru or the nearest spiritual organization. Aren't they always tuned to the receiving channels? Give and yeh shall receive. It is a spiritual truth and reality. As a child, you had no problems with receiving. You always got what you needed and more. And it was easy too. The father might commit a crime, the mother might do menial work, but the child receives its milk. The child is in a state of pure receiving. Credit may be given to the father and mother, but more credit needs to be given to the receiving powers of the child. The child will get its milk with or without its parents.

A rich man offered a Zen master a huge amount of money as donation. The Zen master promptly took the gift, nodded and put the money away safely. The donor was a bit dissatisfied. He had expected a little more appreciation from the master. Not being able to contain himself, he said to the master, "you never praised me enough when I gave you so much?" At this the Zen master smiled and responded with a twinkle in his eye "At least I said Thank You." And as a passing remark he also said, "By the way, you should have thanked me for accepting your gifts." "Because your giving me is meaningless unless I am ready to receive."

And the truth for you is —

You cannot give unless there is someone around to receive and is ready for it.

Are you waiting for that breakthrough in your life? You simply need to open yourself to receive naturally. Train yourself to believing that receiving is good and pure. And the floodgates to receiving will open. And you will see wonderful things and favourable events gushing into the vacuum of your life. This is just like the pipe that is clogged up and water is not coming through. There is water but you are not getting it. You remove the block and water gushes in.

Receiving is being ready. Haven't you heard, "When the disciple is ready the master appears"

The husband although very young had a weak heart and was undergoing treatment. His wife won 500,000 dollars in lottery. Her joy knew no bounds. She wanted to rush home and tell the husband the good news. But then she remembered the doctor's advice against getting him over-excited and called him up. The doctor said, "Listen, this is fantastic news! It must be broken to your husband very gently. Under no circumstance should we allow him to get excited. It is bad for his heart."

Then a plan was worked out in which the doctor would break the news to the husband. The doctor landed up at the couple's home.

After a few civilities, the doctor asked the husband, "How would you react if I told you that your wife won 5000 dollars?" The husband thought a while and said, "I guess, that would help us to make both ends meet this month." The doctor continued, "And how would you feel if she won 50,000?" The husband had a frown and said, "I guess that will help us clear the debts we have on the house and a few other things." Then the doctor said, "And what if it were 500,000?" The husband was getting irritated with his questions. He said, "Listen

Doctor, why are you asking all this?" The Doctor persisted "Tell me how would you feel and what will you do if your wife won 500,000?" The husband answered, "Listen Doc, what I will do is plead with my dear wife and make sure you get 250,000 dollars and then we will have a ball." On hearing this, the Doctor got a heart attack.

The moral of the story is, you have given enough, now it's time to get ready to receive.

Ask and You Will Receive

The real measure of your wealth is how much you'd be worth if you lost all your money.

— Author Unknown

There is great truth in the saying Ask and you will receive. Nature has this beautiful and very valuable golden coin. On one side is, ask and on the other side is receive. Most of you are uncomfortable with this currency of life. Most of you may be very familiar with one side, Asking but not the other. You may be asking your guts out to God, every day but do not see that you have already received. Anyway asking is the greatest tool to activate the power of receiving.

Money Bags was teaching his son the power of asking. He saw a man walking with an elephant. He told his son, "Go ask the man to give his elephant to you." The boy was scared. But the man insisted, "I'm telling you, just do it." Then Money Bags walked over confidently to the man, tapped him on the shoulder and asked, "Uncle, can you give me the elephant for free?" The man simply said, "Here, take it" and appeared relieved.

The outcome of asking is very simple. Either you get what you asked for or you do not. Statistically, this is 50% probability. And that is excellent. When you are debating in your mind about whether or not to ask — whether or not he will give — you can keep doing furious calculations on different levels of probability. I will leave this to the mathematicians within you. As far as I am concerned 100% of my work is done when I ask.

The married and those having young children among you have heard the term, demand feeding of infants advised by doctors. And how does a little baby demand its feed. The baby yells. People generally call this crying. Anyway that signals a flow of milk from the mother. It is perfect harmony. Yelling, call it crying or whatever is the child's language for asking. The baby that cries always gets the milk. It is much later that the child is taught to ask politely without screaming and shouting hoarse.

Asking is instinctive and is a natural process. You are hungry. Your body asks for food. Although, you may be famished you wouldn't want to yell for food at a party. You are taught to be polite and engage in social talk, simply hoping inside that the meal is announced soon. For example, you are invited to a friend's house for lunch or dinner. When your young son feels hungry, he cares nothing about the weather. He pops up the 1000 dollar question totally unafraid, "Aunt, when are you going to serve food?" You may be embarrassed but he is not and most certainly 'Aunt' is not embarrassed either, if they are the kind of friends you ought to be having.

So, take a leaf out of the baby and children's book and ask your customers, "When are you going to pay my money?" You can ask your boss too, "When are you going to increase my salary?"

Ask for your stuck money, ask for help and ask for discounts. Be natural and do not be afraid. There are many situations where there is no hike in the salary of employees for a long time. Most certainly this situation exists because nobody asked for a raise. There are a thousand situations every day where you can practice asking. And the greatness of asking is that it invariably brings more honesty in your life. People generally take cognizance of this and will respect you for it. And most importantly, you will respect your own self.

You have a right to ask. Nobody should be afraid to ask. There is everything to gain and nothing to lose by asking.

Power of Giving

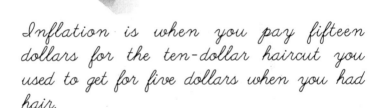

Inflation is when you pay fifteen dollars for the ten-dollar haircut you used to get for five dollars when you had hair.

— Sam Ewing

Friend: "If you have two cars, will you be kind enough to donate one car for the under privileged?"

Golmaal: "Yes for sure."

Friend: "If you have two houses, will you be kind enough to donate one house for the under privileged?"

Golmaal: "Yes surely."

Friend: "If you have two hundred rupees, will you be kind enough to donate one hundred rupees for the under- privileged."

Golmaal: "No, never."

Friend: "What! You can donate a car, a house but can't

donate a mere hundred rupees?"

Golmaal: "Because I don't have a car or a house but I do have two hundred rupees!"

Some don't like to give and many just keep giving all through their lives. Let us simplify and get our perspective right on the aspect of Giving. It has been said that the more you give the more you get in return. This needs to be rephrased into the more you give consciously the more you get in return. One word here or there can make a heaven of a difference. Giving consciously or with awareness is the true giving.

Many participants at the Money Workshop have asked me: Should I give alms to beggars? And what are the factors I should consider before parting away with the money? This is a practical question and surely needs an answer. Let us first look at what people are doing with respect to beggars.

There was a lame beggar, standing on one leg in the hot afternoon. A lady went to him and started chatting with him.

Lady to beggar: "You know how tough life is, and look at you only one leg, you must feel very bad."

Beggar: "Man, such is destiny what to do?"

Lady: "I am sympathetic, but you have at least have a leg. Imagine how worse life could be if you were blind."

Beggar: "Yes, what you say is true; when I was blind, people only gave me counterfeit currency."

Many are spending too much time being offensive. Many can

qualify for a Ph.D in 'Beggarology'. It is really funny when people spend more time and energy in working out categories of beggars.

When life is already complicated why are we complicating it further? Their research says: One should give money to the blind, old or infant beggars. Never give beggars who are healthy or who have all their body parts intact. These are just the basics and many more advanced theories and combinations have been worked out. Each time a beggar appears, a complete analysis is done before parting with money. To top it all, after giving money, they follow the beggar to check if he is using the money properly. Imagine following the beggar, people might wonder who the real beggar is?

Can you understand how much complexity we have created on a beggarly issue?

The correct act of giving is to Give and Forget. The act of giving has to come spontaneously from the heart. Every giving is a personal experience. You should feel nice from within every time you give. Unless this happens, giving is empty and meaningless. Once you have given the money does not belong to you. So what he does with the money is his own choice.

Before giving money or anything else you can think and evaluate carefully whom and what cause to give to. But after you give the act is over. What the other person now does is no concern of yours. The other person is just incidental in the process.

Sadly those who have in plenty don't give, while those who have less give even that away. The rich give to wash away their sins or for securing a place in Heaven. Giving with calculations or expectation has no meaning. It is better not to give in such instances. Giving should arise from a state of abundance rather than guilt or obligation.

Those who don't have enough, it is not necessary to give money always. You can give time, creative ideas or just blessings.

Let every giving arise from the bottom of your heart and enrich your inner being with joy and bliss — a pure state of being.

Have Healthy Savings and Reserves.

Money — Spending
and Saving

Money is like manure. You have to spread it around or it smells.

— J. Paul Getty

Do You Have Prosperity Eyes?

The little money I have — that is my wealth, but the things I have for which I would not take money, that is my treasure.

— Robert Brault

When you look around what do you see? There are skyscrapers alongside huts, five-star hotels along with small eateries and the glitz and glamour of the city against the backdrop of poverty and starvation. The world is full of such stark contrasts. Life can be so black but thanks to our eyes the world appears so colourful. The power of connecting to prosperity or poverty, to abundance or scarcity purely rests in our eyes and mind.

When you look at the items in a window display and your eyes fall on the diamond-encrusted watches, a thought might cross your mind, 'this is not for me.' A very dangerous thought indeed for you have cut the diamond watch out of your life. Similarly you will be shocked with the number of wonderful items that you may have restricted from coming into your life.

When you spot beautiful things, look with awe and wonderment in your eyes. Feel the wow within you. This is like clicking photographs with your camera. This image passes through your being and is registered in your mind. Remember, things are created twice — first in the mind and then in reality.

When you look around and see things,

See all things around with love,

Then all the things that you love,

In your life you will see.

Say wow with feelings to all things that you desire and watch as it magically manifests in your life.

Bite into the Wonders of a Juicy Golden Mango

A bank is a place that will lend you money if you can prove that you don't need it.

— Bob Hope

Imagine that you have a big juicy golden yellow mango. You're just about to bite into it when a thought of its origin crosses your mind.

Some wonderful farmer, many years ago planted a seed. Like rearing a tiny baby, the farmer tended to his mango saplings with love and care. He used the right kind of soil, a large quantity of water, the best of fertilizers and perfect sunlight. His joy knew no bounds as he watched the seed transform first into a tender green sapling and then into a tree. He protected it like his own baby. A few years later, the tree started flowering and bore small raw mangoes. With the passage of time, the mangoes turned ripe and golden. Then, with gentle wrinkled hands the farmer plucked the mangoes, laid them softly over the basket and carried them to town. From the village to the town, from the farmer to the shopkeeper, traversing through unknown destinations over thousands of miles the mango finally reached your super-store. The love and the labour of so many individuals along with total support from the eco-system have all come together to give birth to this lovely mango. You spotted it the next day, paid for it and now it rests in your hands.

As you sink your teeth and bite the mango, you realize that you are lucky to taste the loveliest and juiciest of mangoes.

Just like the mango, everything in life is a culmination of the efforts, love and contribution of many people. Can you ever put a price on the many elements which have gone into the divine creation of the mango? You have taken it so much for granted that you don't realize how expensive it will be to produce even a single mango. And you got it so cheap.

How much will you cherish when you bite a mango and know that its worth is hundreds of thousand rupees. And this is the same with everything that we buy or use.

Next time when you get dressed, wear your watch, grab your mobile phone or travel by car, realize that their essential value is worth a million dollars. Not only will you be able to enjoy all those to the fullest, but also you will stop complaining about the high cost.

The Menu Card Mentality

If you lend someone $20, and never see that person again, it was probably worth it.

— Author Unknown

You go to a restaurant. The first thing thrust on you is a menu card. Most of you will first look towards the right side where the prices are given. Later one turns to look at the left side where the eatables and beverages are listed. You go through the whole menu card and finally order 'idli-wada sambhar,' the same dish you have been having for ages. Thank God! The price of 'idli wada sambhar has not increased too much and is still affordable. The super veggie pizza that you desired to eat was left behind in the menu card, as the price did not fit your pocket.

You want to buy clothes. And in the shop you see items that you like a lot. As you go near you can see the price tag and it sure is exorbitant! So, you have to drop the idea of you being dressed up in that really smart set of clothes. And you pick up some clothes whose price tags don't give you a shock. You travel by second class, because there is no choice of third class.

These are many instances that we come across that have etched a pattern in our lives. You attract the things, which you really don't like, because the best things, that you would like to choose, have dropped out, due to their prices. This later develops into a vicious circle and starts affecting the other areas of your life. You attract a job or a business line, which doesn't really interest you. If there are customers you are not particularly fond of and if things were to go really bad for you, you might end up being miserable.

To break this dangerous cycle, you have to do something right now. Take some conscious decisions based on liking and not on pricing. Look at the left hand side of the menu card, give some importance to what your likes and preferences are. You will soon see a fresh whiff of fragrance in your life. Slowly and steadily, you will start appearing attractive on the outside, since you're feeling attractive from the inside. Earn well and spend it well. Use good quality things and take pride in doing so. You will soon start experiencing a whole reversal. You will start attracting things that you like. Settle only for the best things in life. Lead a first class life.

All I Want Is Everything

Money can't buy happiness, but it can buy you the kind of misery you prefer.

— Author Unknown

"Spending gives me the jitters," "I just hate spending," "I spend money and then feel very guilty," "bills, bills everywhere, but no money to spare," are some of the comments that one hears on spending.

Two friends were chatting about endless unnecessary expenses.

One friend to the other: "Last evening, dust entered into my wife's eyes and I had to unnecessarily spend at the eye specialist."

The other friend said, "Man you are so lucky, last evening a diamond entered into my wife's eyes and you know how much I had to spend!"

Did you not ever wish that all things in the world were free?

On the other hand "I just love spending," "Give me any

amount of money and I will spend it in just a moment," are what many subscribe to. So, whenever you need to spend your own money, it is natural for you to have a internal debate "should I — shouldn't I?" Many of you can get tired with all that mental activity, give up the debate and decide to spend with any justification you can find. Your indecision to spend or not to spend could be as serious as Hamlet's indecision, to be or not to be

When you go to a shopping mall, there are carts and small shopping baskets. Watch out, the shopaholics unconsciously will always pick up the huge cart. Inside the mall every product speaks the same language — 'Pick me up,' 'take me home.' The shopaholics hand will move automatically, pick up the product and drop it into the cart. All this takes no more than a few seconds. The shopping cart keeps getting filled by the minute — like water gushing in when the dam gates are opened. Somewhere in the corner is a product lost to eternity which no one notices. Even the shopkeeper has forgotten about its existence. Here comes our shopaholic who not only notices it, but also pounces on it and puts it into his cart.

Lugging his cart he goes to the cashier who has a smile on his face, for he loves such people. Smilingly he hands him a big fat bill. Now money gushes out of the wallet, like water gushing out of a tap. He comes home and thrusts into his wife's hand a number of plastic bags filled with goodies — "Darling, all this is for you." The wife takes her own sweet time to rummage through all the items. She discovers that her husband has got her everything except what she wanted. This is unconscious and unplanned spending, where you lose control to the temptation of the products.

Mrs. Malamaal: "Can you tell me how much you spend out of 100% of your income."

Mrs. Golmaal: "I spend 30% on food, 30% on clothing, 40% on shelter, 50% on entertainment."

Mrs. Malamaal: "What! That makes it 150%!"

Mrs Golmaal: "Yes. I have improved, earlier it used to be 200%."

Learn the art of spending money wisely and consciously. If one side of the coin is spending the other side is earning. One should not hate, fear or feel guilty while spending. The purpose of money is to circulate, and the more it circulates the more you become prosperous. Look into your life, how dull and drab it would be — if money is still in the form of paper, metal or a plastic card. Each time you spend, you get to enjoy the benefits of the products and services. The next time you enter into a mall, plan what you want to purchase. Don't be too tempted by the lure of products screaming 'buy me, take me home.'

Remember the road to prosperity has many parking lots — mindless shopping is one of them.

Principle of Maximum Extraction

Money will buy you a pretty good dog,
but it won't buy the wag of his tail.
— Henry Wheeler Shaw

A family of four is at an upmarket ice-cream parlour. The parents are obsessed with the right hand side of the menu, worried about the dizzying prices of the ice-creams. The children, on the other hand look happily at the left hand side. True life pictures of different types of ice-creams dance before their eyes. The father is looking on resignedly. He knows his innocent children have the unconscious knack of choosing the most expensive items anyway. After a bit of bickering interspersed with parental advice on why too much chocolate is bad for the teeth, they place the orders.

It is interesting to know what is going on in the minds as they wait for their ice-creams.

The father keeps pushing back thoughts of how expensive things are, how much the bill is going to be and whether he should tip the waiter. He also thinks of how the money saved on ice-cream could have gone on to fund a couple of important things. The mother too is thinking of where she could learn about the recipes and fancy toppings on the ice-cream. She is consumed by thoughts of how, if she had bought the ingredients separately, she could have made enough ice-cream within that same amount for an entire month. The children's overwhelming question, which they don't hesitate to ask is, "When is that waiter going to get the ice-cream?"

A minute later beautifully garnished ice-creams arrive, snapping everyone out of their reverie. All that the father can see now is the bill looming large. All that the mother sees is the cosmetics she could have bought with the same amount. Arrival of the ice-cream brings real joy on the childrens faces. Then all the four relish the ice-cream.

Now, here is my question. Who do you think extracted maximum satisfaction in the above episode? I guess all of you will be unanimous in saying, 'Undoubtedly, the children.'

Once you decide to spend, all that remains in your hands is the power to extract the maximum from it. So the next time your money decision is taken, be like a child again and extract the maximum.

Bargain to Glory

In the old days a man who saved money was a miser; nowadays he's a wonder.

— Author Unknown

When it comes to bargaining there are two kinds of people: one who bargains to the fullest and the other who never bargains. Bargaining is a good skill to possess in the money world. The world of money is all about negotiations and bargaining is one of them. Let us look closer at what happens in bargaining.

Let us assume there are two parties involved, A and B. A is the shopkeeper and B is the customer. The basic premise is that A would do anything to prevent bargaining from happening and B should do everything to get the bargaining in his/her favour. Bargaining has to do more with protection of 'Personal Powers' than with 'Money'. Make it a playful affair. Be always cool and composed while bargaining. When you are good at bargaining, you achieve two things; you improve your interpersonal skills and you also save your money. Money saved leads to money earned.

Santa told Banta, "Arrey yaar! I'm going to Delhi this summer with my family. Tell me where I should shop."

Banta, with great enthusiasm said, "Arrey boss. Delhi is a great shopping place. Umm, only be careful about the pricing. Bargain heavily and ask for half the price of what the shopkeeper offers. Chalo! Have a great trip. See you soon!"

Santa reached Delhi and was shopping early that morning, when his eyes got fixed to the latest music system. He badly wanted it at his place, so he decided to check on the price. The shopkeeper had just then finished his morning prayers and gave Santa a beaming welcome.

Santa: "What's the price of the music system over the shelf there Bhai saab?"

Shopkeeper: "It is priced at Rs. 10,000 rupees but since you are my first customer I shall give you a thousand rupees discount. I will give it for Rs 9000."

Santa remembered Banta's advice he said: "I will give you only 4500 rupees."

Shopkeeper: "Bhai saab, let us settle at Rs. 8000."

Santa: "I will give only Rs. 4000."

Shopkeeper: "Neither yours nor mine, let me pack the music system for just Rs. 7000 only for you, Sir."

Santa: "I will give only Rs. 3500."

Shopkeeper: (Very irritated) "Hey Mister, why don't you take it for free?"

Santa: "Good, pack two of them."

There are two powerful techniques in Bargaining

1. Positioning Technique:

If the shopkeeper says the price is Rs. 9000, then place a position far below what he could expect. For example, you could place a position at Rs. 4000. Now he has to pull the price from Rs. 4000 upwards, the price where you have placed your position. He could pull it to Rs. 6000. You could place another position at Rs. 4500, which he will pull upwards, and the final strike price will be around Rs. 5000.

2. The Gramophone Broken Record:

Have you ever listened to old gramophone records especially when they are worn out or scratched? They keep on playing the same sound track again and again. You could use this same strategy in bargaining. Keep saying the same sentence in the same manner again and again. For example: "I will pay only Rs. 3000." Now it does not matter what the other person says because you have discovered your broken record, which is, "I will pay only Rs 3000."

The secret of our mind is that ...*It can hear any sentence up to a maximum seven times before its resistance is broken...* So by repeating this sentence again and again the other person succumbs and yields to your demand.

Finally the big rule of bargaining is:

Always bargain with others, but when it comes to your products and services, don't allow bargaining to happen.

Happy Bargaining!

The World Is Out to Give You Money

Let us more and more insist on raising funds of love, of kindness, of understanding, of peace. Money will come if we seek first the Kingdom of God — the rest will be given.

— Mother Teresa

Today the world has so much to offer in terms of material wealth that it is incredibly tempting. Because of this seduction, we are very likely to be tempted to borrow more than our payback capacity.

Debt comes in different garbs — credit cards, personal loans etc. Every bank and credit card company wants you to take money from them. Some of you might have pre-approved drafts sent to you. Taking a loan is made so simple. Most advertisements say: Loan without hassles, no proofs of income, easy paper work, please call at this number. And you might be at this point of time being very tempted.

Just because at this moment you think you are earning enough to repay a loan doesn't make taking a loan the best option. The organization you borrow from makes loan taking hugely attractive because they want the interest. Don't be a fool. If you must borrow, use the facility in moderation and make the distinction. Borrow for investment not for consumption — a house, education, that's investment. A holiday to South of France, that's consumption. A sure sign of excessive borrowing is when you encounter tremendous mental pressure that builds up within you causing you to feel cornered.

The debt trap is a death trap. Steer clear of it.

Be Neither a Borrower nor a Lender

By the time I have money to burn, my fire will have burnt out.

— *Author Unknown*

When a beggar comes to you one fine morning, look at how disturbed you become because he is asking for money. This scene is no different when you go for borrowing money from friends or relatives.

Beware — The most dangerous phenomenon in the money world is borrowing. And even more dangerous is, borrowing from friends and relatives. Borrowing money from friends and relatives is a reflection of your own incompetence. Like cancer, it spreads and destroys relationships and reputation.

Borrowing can waste not just your present money but can also destroy your future money. This occurs when you borrow heavily and it spins out of control.

Living beyond ones means or mishandling of Money — one can be put into this pitiable situation. Your relatives and friends may part with money because of their inability to say NO. They may be obligated to you for some other reason and may thus not want to refuse you the money. They may perhaps want similar favours from you in future and thus want to do so. Or they just want to get rid of you and have no choice but to pay.

The borrowing habit quickly turns into a chronic illness and one is unable to get rid of it. You tend to build all sorts of stories to fool your own conscious mind. Deep down in your mind and heart you know all this is simply a concoction of your fertile imagination, but you are unable to do anything to fight it. One leads to another and before you know it, you have already been consumed by the huge monster created by none other than yourself. You lose your sense of self-respect, you become immune to taunts, criticism, jokes and jibes aimed at you, sometimes even dirty looks.

Congratulations, you have become a thick-skinned borrower.

Mr. Compulsive Borrower consults a psychiatrist: "Doctor, I face a constant struggle with my ethics and conscience. And you know how tough the money world is? Whenever I borrow my conscience really bothers me. I feel heavy with the burden of my conscience"

Doctor: "Good man I do understand your problem, you want me to build a stronger willpower for you, right?"

Mr. Compulsive Borrower: "Oh! No, Doctor. I want you to weaken my conscience."

If you want to avoid losing your face, blindly follow the time-tested formula — **Neither a borrower nor a lender be**.

Retire Young

The best way for a person to have happy thoughts is to count his blessings and not his cash.

— Author Unknown

Visualize a day in your life when you could afford to do all those things you loved or wanted to do. It could be to keep on reading books, playing with your children, dancing in the rain or just lazing around. Deep down we all look forward to such fantasies. Few can make it really happen. If someone, somewhere is making it possible then why not you? Though picture perfect, you can have your days, months and years in the sun.

One evening, I was observing an ant. It was carrying a grain of sugar much bigger than its weight and slowly inching its way. Many a time, the sugar crystal slipped. But the ant was persistent and never gave up. It carried the sugar with slow yet steady steps till it finally reached its destination. Again it came for the next grain of sugar. For days together it would do just this. This ant was smart and knew how to take care of itself. It now had more than enough to see through the rains. It had built reserves, which it could always bank on.

Can't we take a page from this ant's life? If we can build huge reserves that can see us for one lifetime our task is achieved. If money flow in your life is completely stopped, yet you have cash reserves to take care of all your needs for one lifetime (estimate a life span of 80 years to be on the safe side), and you never need to work again for Money, then you have a choice to retire completely. Or you may also choose to work because you love it.

Many of us believe that such a life is meant only for the super rich. And the super rich who can afford to do this today don't take the plunge. They are scared of themselves, scared of the world which might criticize, scared of pure happiness and scared of the many imagined and unimagined things that could happen. Or in the mechanical way of day to day running, they simply have not given a thought to this.

Money Techniques

The best month to have money is December, some of the other months are October, April, August, March, May, January, July, September, November, June and February.

— Suresh Padmanabhan

Have LSD to Be Successful in Your Money World

If you owe the bank $100 that's your problem. If you owe the bank $100 million, that's the bank's problem.

— *J.P. Getty*

Some of you may ask, "What?" "LSD?" Don't be scared. My prescriptions are not for medication. LSD is acronym for **Laughing, Singing and Dancing**.

LSD was traditionally part and parcel of the activities of human beings around the world for ages. This is the natural state of human beings to be full of energy and capable of peak performance always.

It is not that you should be in LSD only when you have money. Actually, it should be the reverse. You should be in LSD always so that your potential to make money is high.

Have you observed infants and children? They are always bubbling with energy. It takes many adults to handle just a small infant. Adults get tired keeping pace with kids. Where do you think they get so much energy? They are always in a natural state of Laughing, Singing and Dancing. Adults seem to have lost that naturalness somewhere. They are deprived of life's vital energies. The zest, sparkle and enthusiasm all seem to be missing.

Reconnect with the child within you — have a regular dose of LSD and you will find yourself rejuvenated.

Joy of Contentment

Money won't create success, the freedom to make it will.

— Nelson Mandela

Look at the following numbers and what do you notice?

1 2 3 5 6 7 8 9 0

Many of you would immediately say that number 4 is missing.

You always think of what is missing in real life.

That is why when money is there you do not bother about it and when it is missing, it suddenly hits you. When your teeth are there you do not bother about them. The day you lose one, your tongue keeps searching for it in the blank space.

When you are in your own country, you take it for granted. And when you migrate to another you miss your country, your food, your people, and your language very much.

Look at these numbers again. What do you notice?

1 2 3 5 6 7 8 9 0

Do not tell me again that the number 4 is missing. Have you not noticed all those numbers 1, 2, 3, 5, 6, 7, 8, 9 and 0?

When you keep thinking about what is missing, the reality and beauty of that which is present has been missing. The reality is always what exists, and not what is missing. In short, you are a foreigner in the alien land — a mere second grade citizen. Missing is like a big hole, a bottomless pit and whatever you put into it, it cannot fill it.

You buy a big car and for a short time you love it. Then, your neighbour gets the latest model and soon you start finding faults with your car. The car that you loved so much now starts looking dowdy and boring to you. It no longer holds the charm it once held. Your mind is already looking at replacing it with the latest one. Similarly all through life you will be unrelentingly searching for missing things.

Connect well to whatever you have and you will experience expansion and contentment in our being. When you look at your car, relate the wonderful service it has given you. Connect to the joy you had when you bought it. Look back at the many wonderful rides you have had with your family in it. And though old, it still serves you so well. It takes you to office and does not break down. Can you comprehend how much it cares for you? But do you care for it? If your car or any other gadget that you have is not serving you well, it doesn't mean that it is bad or faulty, rather this indicates that you are not taking good care of it.

All things around us have intrinsic energy. Stay in tune with the energy within things and there is cooperation for the best results. Express gratitude for people and things around you. Everything, from people to things, needs your love and gratitude as much as you need them. When you appreciate and are grateful, God/Universe decides to reward you with many more wonderful things and supportive people.

Don't you like to go to places where you are respected? Why should the universal energy not do the same? The state of being content is very different from a state of being devoid of desire. Do not confuse yourself. Desire is essential for growth in our money world but it has to come with contentment with whatever we have. Desire does not necessarily mean discontentment.

A man built a two-room apartment for himself. He attained prosperity and found his soul mate. Now he wanted to grow as a family. He thanked the Superior Power for his present happiness and prayed for a larger space. He had a bachelor friend who wanted to buy his present house. He sold his apartment happily and now moved into a larger apartment with his bride.

Express gratitude and appreciate all things that you have. Be it shoes that you wear or that piece of diamond-studded gold jewellery or your washing machine and then you will discover the joy of contentment.

When Every Word Matters

Successful people make money. It's not that people who make money become successful, but that successful people attract money. They bring success to what they do.

— *Wayne Dyer*

It was a cold evening. I was traveling by train. The train stopped at a station and a man boarded in with a can of coffee. He started moving around the compartments yelling, "Coffee, coffee, coffee." He was a vendor. None of the passengers bothered to even look at him. Not a single cup of coffee was sold. Mumbling to himself, the disappointed man got down at the next station.

Then another vendor, a young guy with a sparkle in his eye, boarded the train. In a sing song manner, he started saying, "Hot coffee, hot coffee" emphasizing the word hot. This stirred the interest of the sleepy passengers. The word hot penetrated through their disinterest and struck a note in tune with the warmth they were seeking. Many started ordering. The young guy cheerfully served them steaming cups of hot coffee. Within no time the container was empty. He got down at the next station with his pockets jingling and overflowing with money.

All the difference in this entire story was made by one word 'hot'. It brought out the actual warmth that the passengers were waiting to experience (but were perhaps unaware of). The second vendor came in at the right time and said the right thing! Never underestimate the power of the written or spoken word. Every word spoken can take you towards money or away from it.

Ask yourself, "In my job, work or profession; am I using the right words?"

What Legacy Would You Like to Leave Behind?

If all the economists were laid end to end, they'd never reach a conclusion.

— George Bernard Shaw

A pile of debts for your dear ones to wallow in?

Unsettled and unfinished business?

Financial burdens that will haunt your loved ones for the rest of their lives?

A chaotic and unclear will is bound to cause the kind of epic in fighting that would put even the Mahabharata to shame.

A badly-documented record of transactions, both, the past as well as the current, all lying in a muddle in your bottom sock drawer, would frustrate and confuse even Sherlock Holmes!

The fact is that all you ever did in life was keep your nose to the grindstone and your shoulder to the till, not having a single moment to bask in life's sundry joys. And you did not have the time to keep your papers intact. One of the key areas in the money world is proper handing over of money and assets to your dependents. Especially so when there is more than enough money or assets but everything is undocumented. Also, a person close to you should be aware of all your Money Transactions. Many people are so secretive that they don't want others, even their dear ones, to know about their complete money picture. Death can come anytime so it is essential to be prepared with the accounts well in advance.

While alive do not create a mess with money so much that it will cause trouble to your loved ones later.

Porky Pig and Useful Cow were arguing about who was the more useful one amongst the two of them. Porky Pig was saying that it is more useful than the Useful Cow because it sacrifices itself for human beings.

Useful Cow said to Porky Pig; "Dear Porky Pig, you're useful only when dead, while I give milk every day." It is better to be like the Useful Cow i.e. be useful while you are alive.

My mother is an excellent example of people with a giving attitude. Even with her limited resources she has a generous heart and often gives most of what she has. Her simple philosophy is, "it is better to help others than spending huge money on unnecessary rituals." According to Hindu tradition, rituals form a part of life, right from the birth in the family to a death in one. In fact, the 'shraadh' ritual is performed for 13 days after the death of a person for liberation of the soul.

You live only once. Lead your money life clearly whilst alive. When you die be sure to have left behind your clear money footprints for your loved ones to follow. Your absence will be sorely missed but they will bless you for your far-sightedness and clarity.

Do You Eat Bricks, Cement and Gold?

Of the billionaires I have known, money just brings out the basic traits in them. If they were jerks before they had money, they are simply jerks with a billion dollars.

— Warren Buffett

Some people are quite imbalanced with their money. As money keeps coming in they go on purchasing real estate, land, gold and ornaments etc. Sometimes this becomes so obsessive that they don't even have small liquid cash for day-to-day expenses. This is real craziness. On paper they have huge assets, but lead a beggarly life. They can earn the title of 'Poor little Rich Beggar.'

There has to be a proper balance between Assets and Liquid Cash. This depends on your own needs and comforts. You cannot avoid paying for what you have bought or used, can you? Can you pay by cement and bricks at the hotel when you run short of cash? When the laundry and milkman come for their due payments, can you ask them to take a small part of your land?

Such people create another big problem for themselves and their family. They are never willing to dispose off their assets to run their day-to-day expenses. They will borrow money, starve, keep electricity and phone bills pending, not pay for children's school fees, and keep struggling day in and day out.

Understand that we have created the assets for ourselves, so it is perfect to utilize these assets when it is necessary. The other situation where you need to dispose of your assets could be when unforeseen events strike you or when you are in a deep financial crisis. It is wisest to sell whatever assets you have created, though it might be painful to let them go. An incomplete past money issue can be a drain on your energy and personal powers.

Many times the idea to change your decision, if delayed, will cost you years of running a bad business and will prove to be a costly mistake more than anything else.

Every new creation is born out of destruction. Do firmly believe that you can always recreate what you created once. It is better to start on a clean slate again than to start from a mess. It takes a lot more effort to clean the mess than to start afresh.

Welcome to a World of Diaries

Do not value money for any more nor any less than its worth; it is a good servant but a bad master.

— Alexandre Dumas fils, Camille, 1852

Diaries simplify one's work, be it regarding your monetary transactions or your line of work. You can keep a system of diaries that will simplify your task concerning money. These systems will also help you to understand money, thereby eliminating human factors like laziness, procrastination or simply a 'careless' attitude.

Daily Diary: This is a list of work that you need to do each day. At the start of the day, when you plan out the tasks and write it down in your diary, you can work as though the task is already completed. For example: If a cheque is to be picked up from a client and deposited in the bank, you could note it down as: Got the cheque in hand and deposited it into the bank.

Daily Account Diary: This is a diary where you can write your daily income and expenses. This would account every rupee coming in and going out.

Ideas Diary: The brain is an excellent sponge, soaking in every little stimulus for future use at some point in time. Along with our regular duties and activities, it is also important to cultivate an inner ear to listen to our mind and the ideas it is capable of generating. If we do not put these ideas into writing, they might simply evaporate out of our lives and a powerful idea could get wasted.

An idea is the first step or seed to a new reality. As you get ideas just write them down, without judging them either on their workability or on their being small or big. At the end of the day review all the ideas and check those, which have a meaning for your life. Then look into that idea and very soon a very powerful path will emerge.

Actions Diary: Daily ask yourself what money action did I take today? Whenever you take an action on any area of money just write it down. This way you will become more action oriented. And remember that only actions get you results.

Desire Diary: To desire is not wrong, in fact it is more like the energy drink that drives you with more zeal and determination towards its goals. Let your desires be clearly written as well as putting them down visually (through a photo, cut-out of a magazine or a drawing). Keep expanding on this regularly by pasting in more of your desires and by going through your desire diary every day. You will soon see many desires manifested in reality.

Recover Your Stuck Money

Most people work just hard enough not to get fired and get paid just enough money not to quit.

— George Carlin

Dhanraj once met Somu in the park while he was taking a walk. Somu enquired of Dhanraj, "How are you? Have you recovered all your stuck money?" Dhanraj happily informed him that he had indeed recovered all of it.

Somu asked him how he managed it so fast. Dhanraj invited him home the next day, "Come over to my place tomorrow if you want to meet the person who has helped me in this"

Somu could not suppress his curiosity and naturally landed up at Dhanraj's place the next day. Dhanraj called out 'Jibunga'. Somu was waiting for a martial arts specialist. Instead, he saw a three hundred pound gorilla walking towards him and his friend introduced him to his money collector.

Dhanraj then spoke about his difficult times when he was simply unable to recover the moneys people had borrowed from him. No matter what he did, he was unable to solve this problem. So he thought of a novel idea and got Jibunga the gorilla to do this for him. From then on, things got better every day. He simply had to write a note with the name of the person who owed him money and the amount and send Jibunga for a short visit to his place.

There was not a single instance when Jibunga returned empty-handed. Somu was very happy and asked Dhanraj if he could borrow Jibunga to recover his own dues.

Dhanraj obliged. Jibunga went with his friend and collected the dues for him. But, one day somu came to Dhanraj in desperation. "Your Jibunga collected all the money for me but I'm not able to **recover** it from him!"

Stuck money is an issue of your past. It is a messy and sticky issue. You lend money and the borrower doesn't pay you back. It is very difficult to chase unpaid money especially since you have your own affairs to manage. Besides, one does feel humiliated chasing one's own money. Maybe you've tried to recover it for a while and then given up the attempt completely. But whatever you do, do not give up on what is rightfully yours.

Take another look at this issue; after all, it is your money. Take the process of recovery like a game so that it eases the burden on your mind. To start with make a list of the names of people who owe you money, along with the amounts due in order of ease of recovery. Now make a firm resolution to ask; ask and ask powerfully.

Ask annoyingly, ask persistently, ask angrily, ask with a roar — but ask. Whatever you do, don't meow like a scared street cat.

Ask with the clear objective of recovering your money. And if that doesn't work, don't give up. Just re-work strategies to ensure that your money is recovered.

Enact a recovery drama that will really work wonders for you. It could range from showing desperation, tugging at the emotional heart strings, threatening bad publicity or just plonking yourself on his doorstep and not budging till you get your dues. You could also look at alternative ways of family members, if you think that would make him vulnerable. Do make sure you do not get into trouble while trying to recover your money. If he is unable to pay cash, then look at alternatives of a barter deal in terms of some service or commodity that he could offer, to make up for the money that he owes.

Do not overdo any attempt to recover your money. People react to such pressure in different ways and therefore it is essential for me to warn you against taking any aggressive steps towards this goal.

Account for every recovery made by documenting your success story. The biggest transformation is when the pattern within you is reversed. Now you don't attract people who need to borrow. This could be a big feather in your cap.

To Do:

1. Write down names of people who have borrowed money from you and the amount borrowed.

2. Write down all actions you had taken and the date.

3. Write all actions that you wish to take now.

4. Write amount recovered and date of recovery.

How to Avoid Money Getting Stuck in the Future

I'm so poor I can't even pay attention.

— Ron Kittle

Awareness and assertiveness are the two attributes that you need, to prevent your money being stuck. Let's look at a process to protect your money in future.

Consider that an acquaintance comes to borrow money from you. You need to put on your spectacles of awareness instantly and ask him why he needs the money. After verifying the genuineness of his need you have two options available — Say yes or refuse straight away.

Somewhere deep down if you feel that he does not have the capacity to pay back or his proposal is not financially sound, then say, NO with a high degree of assertion. Now is the time to utilize some of your 101 ways of saying NO. Some examples are, "I have year-marked my funds for something else," "I have just lent money to someone yesterday" and so on. You might feel uncomfortable saying NO but understand that it's better to feel bad right now rather than feeling worse later.

On the other hand, if you decide to part with some money then add some safety checks. The first is to delay the payment asking him to come back later. Chances are, having been grilled in the first place and realizing money is not easy to come by, he might not return.

If he does return, don your safety glasses once more and check if you can support him in any other way apart from giving him money. It could be anything — an idea, a contact etc.

Often we feel that giving money is the best way to help. But it is not so. The so-called help might actually turn into a disaster for him, converting him into a parasite because he gets it so easily.

If eventually you do give him the money, then prior to that ask when and how he intends to return it. Ensure what he says is actually possible.

Finally give him less than what he has asked for i.e. 50 to 60 percent of the sum he has asked for. This is an easy process to follow and it ensures that your money is not stuck.

Remember that nobody, other than you, can protect your money.

Money and Mysteries

Money is like an arm or leg —use it or lose it.

— Henry Ford

When the Black Cat Took Your Money Away

I try to give to the poor people for love what the rich could get for money. No, I wouldn't touch a leper for a thousand pounds; yet I willingly cure him for the love of God.

— Mother Teresa

Many people have asked me this question, what to do in certain situations like, "If a black cat crosses my path it is bad luck, so what should I do?"

Please follow the following instructions very carefully. When a black cat crosses your path, go back exactly two steps, allow the cat to cross the road. Wait in silence for 120 seconds. Then put your right foot, always the right foot first and then the left. Walk three steps ahead ...look to the right and then towards your left...see if there are any more cats coming.

Follow all the above instructions only:

If you are a Mouse.

For ages man has lost or forgotten his God-given powers. So many superstitions bind him. He has become weak. He has stopped reasoning and questioning the number of crazy superstitions that he follows. Are any of these stupidities even remotely connected to losing or gaining money?

Let us live a dignified life and use at least some percentage of the God-given human powers to improve the quality of life.

What Has the Future in Store for Me?

It is not the employer who pays the wages. Employers only handle the money. It is the customer who pays the wages.

— Henry Ford

I remember a nice summer evening when I was walking down the street. I happened to see a man looking very famished standing in a corner. He had a parrot in a cage that looked impoverished too. One often sees such a scene in many parts of India where people set shop for predicting the future with the help of a parrot — trained to pick certain cards that predict the future.

Just then a black shining car came along and a rich looking man got down from the car. He went straight to the man with the parrot. I could see a hint of glow in the poor man's face at the prospect of getting some money or may be food after a long time. He must have been very pleased, because such people are not so lucky all the time.

The parrot promptly hopped out of the cage, picked up a card and handed it over to his master. The futurologist peered at the card in a very thoughtful state. All the while the rich man was eager to know what was in store for him.

I was looking at this scene in amazement. Probably this rich man must have got tired by the wrong predictions given to him by palmists, astrologers, numerologists that he had turned to the parrot's predictions as a last resort. And the poor parrot, which was itself trapped in a cage, was perhaps wondering as to when his own imprisonment was to come to an end. Was it not a cruel joke played by destiny.

From times immemorial, everything from tea leaves to rolling dice, from palm and face reading, numbers, planetary positions and parrots have been used to support the cause of predicting the future of mankind.

The number 9 was predicted as Money Baba's lucky number. It was supposed to turn everything in his favour.

So, on the 9th of September (the 9th month), Money Baba wore a T shirt with the number 9 printed on it. Got out of his car with a fancy number plate reading number 9, went to the derby and bet 9 lacs on the number 9 horse. The race started and Money Baba stretched his neck to see the outcome and was thoroughly disappointed on losing all the money because the horse came 9th.

Many want to find out when their dark days will be over and many want to find out how long will their bright and prosperous days last.

There is no harm in consulting experts who have years of mastery in the subject. A true master will be someone who will create a future for you, rather than predict it. He would do this by sowing the right words and right thoughts in your mind.

The bigger danger is when whatever is predicted actually starts working. Then you are trapped forever. Your mind then starts subconsciously depending on such predictions for decisions related to most aspects of your life. Moreover, you lose your personal powers and the glint in your eyes too.

Reading your sun signs first thing in the morning newspaper is a sure sign of addiction. Please do realize your mind is more receptive to accept negative thoughts and does not easily register the positive thoughts.

Why don't we understand that the universe does not intend our future be known, therefore it has kept it hidden from us. Imagine how dull your life would be when you know your future. Every well-lived present is a sure sign of the bright future.

Good Luck, Bad Luck and the Russian Roulette

If advertisers spent the same amount of money on improving their products as they do on advertising then they wouldn't have to advertise them.

— Will Rogers

Most of us give the word 'luck' different connotations even without understanding what luck really is. We often hear statements such as, "I am lucky," "I am not lucky," "This is Good Luck" and this is "Bad Luck".

You say that luck is bad when things are not going your way on the money front. It appears that you just have these two kinds of stickers and your job is to stick these on the conveyer belt of life in your mind.

At one time, a mummified rabbit's foot was considered to be a charm for good luck in civilized society. Was it the poor rabbit's good luck or bad, when it lost its life and the foot? When you put a good luck label on anything, you put in your energy and power on the thing. Every time you use the Good Luck label you lose your own personal powers.

It is worse using the Bad Luck sticker. Here, you shirk away from your own responsibility. And this is falling into a trap that you may actually like. Then, you think you need not take responsibility for the failure and attribute it to luck.

It is like the case of the man playing Russian roulette for excitement. A potentially lethal game of chance in which participants place a single bullet in a revolver, spin the cylinder, place the muzzle against their head and pull the trigger. Is it his Good Luck if the bullet does not end the game or Bad Luck if it does? Anyway, why play the game at all?

Life fires situations at you at point blank range. It does not ask before firing. And because we do not like life's ways does not mean it will stop firing. The only control you have is to respond sensibly rather than react foolishly.

Good luck and Bad luck labels that you stick on things or events can trap you for a lifetime.

When you remove the words Good Luck and Bad Luck from the dictionary of your life you will truly be liberated.

Money
and
Family

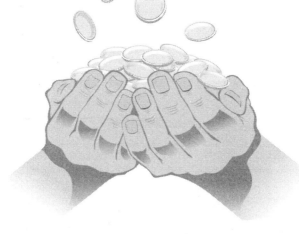

Money is not only important from birth to death but also beyond.

— Suresh Padmanabhan

Salutations to the Indian Homemaker

Run for your life from any man who tells you that money is evil. That sentence is the leper's bell of an approaching looter.

— Ayn Rand

The night is about to give way to the first rays of the golden sun. A few moments and it will be morning as yet, but the lady of the house has risen. She has finished sweeping the verandah and is mopping the house with water. She is singing a wonderful prayer to herself and celebrating the new dawn. She waters the sacred *tulsi* plant and using coloured powder draws a *rangoli* on the floor.

She moves to the inner rooms and tidies the house. She takes a bath and comes into the prayer room. The mood is somber and sacred. She decorates it with flowers, lights a *diya* (lamp) and burns some incense sticks. She prays for the welfare of her husband, children and family members. The whole atmosphere is now radiating with bliss and divinity. The woman of the house has indeed transformed a house of four walls into a home. She has made her house so divine that Goddess Lakshmi (who symbolizes wealth and prosperity) is happy to shower all her blessings on her.

Women contribute whole-heartedly and selflessly to the household. Their love for their husbands and their children surpasses the love they have for themselves. They are home-makers and ought to be addressed likewise.

She takes good care of the house, children, cooking and other mundane activities. Those women who are ambitious but don't compromise on their role as a mother or as a wife, are especially fantastic.

Now the man of the house can focus and use his entire energy to create money and wealth. She has an equal responsibility in the wealth creating activity of the family.

It is therefore widely believed that for a home to experience the bounty of wealth, prosperity and abundance, the woman of the house (the Lakshmi) has to be happy and content.

The Big Fight — Office v/s Home

So you think that money is the root of all evil. Have you ever asked what is the root of all money?

— Ayn Rand

Money Baba was a highly successful and happy man. His close friend and office colleague Chinta Mohan was envious of him and wanted to know his secret. One day he approached Money Baba and told him that he would like to stay with him for a day. Money Baba readily agreed.

That day was hectic. Things just did not go well in the office for Money Baba. He had lot of pending issues and problems to solve. After office, both left for Money Baba's house. Just before entering the house, Money Baba did something weird, which Chinta Mohan noticed. He symbolically hung a bag onto a invisible nail outside his house and then entered.

After that all the worries and tension that he had carried from the office just disappeared. He was happily playing with his children. His wife was also happy because he helped her in the kitchen. The whole family was joyous and celebrating together a very ordinary day.

The next day, again Chinta Mohan observed that Money Baba did something. He went and picked up his symbolic bag from the invisible nail and started walking towards his office. On reaching the office he became focused and engrossed in solving the problems and issues he was faced with.

Curious Chinta Mohan asked Money Baba about the weird bag-hanging act.

Money Baba replied that when he went home he hung the bag outside, symbolizing that he did not want to carry the burden of the office worries into his house.

Next day he picked up the bag to remind him that the issues of the office were important and needed to be tackled. Therefore, he did not want to carry his home into the office. Solutions to those issues were found easily with rejuvenated strength. That was the secret of his success.

The problem is people carry the home to office and their office to the home.

This spillover results in inefficiency at the workplace and an unhappy family at home. Both the vital areas of life work and family get badly affected. How nice it would be if we came to office and meditated for 5 to 10 minutes. This way we will be starting the office energetically on a clean slate. The same thing needs to be done on the house front also.

It is time to have a clear demarcation between work and family.

A Dinner with a Difference

When I chased after money, I never had enough. When I got my life on purpose and focused on giving of myself and everything that arrived into my life, then I was prosperous.

— Wayne Dyer

Imagine the entire family seated around the dinner table sharing a beautiful moment of togetherness. You then get into a conversation on money. How interesting it would be to know that your wife picked up a great bargain. How delighted you'd be if your children had saved up money in their piggy bank. How elated they would be to know that you asked for your raise and also got it. There should be fair, open and transparent money talks that are unbiased and non-critical.

Thus, the whole family learns about money at the dinner table and there is a strong bonding amongst them. It should be a cause for applause and celebration when any member of your family handles money wisely and consciously. Now each member of the family looks forward to his next dinner where he can share with the others his wonderful money achievements. With every dinner this money consciousness can bloom because of the collective consciousness. Unknown to you this triggers many happy events that will come your way.

The family that dines and discusses money together grows together.

Money
and
Organization

Money is usually attracted, not pursued.

— Jim Rohn

Moving Up the Value Chain — Cucumber Theory

Money is only a tool. It will take you wherever you wish, but it will not replace you as the driver.

— Ayn Rand

This is the story of an extraordinary cucumber. Once upon a time in a small village, there lived a number of cucumbers. There was one among them that was the brightest and the smartest. Every day, all the other cucumbers gathered to listen to his wisdom. One day he taught them the wisdom of value addition and pricing.

If the cucumber is in the farm, people just pluck them for free. The cucumber starts moving up the value chain when it goes into the market and is then sold by the kilos. Now the pricing is Re.1/- in the market. A vendor purchases this cucumber, slices it, adds salt and spices and then it is sold in the train for Rs.3-.

Now an hotelier purchases the cucumber for his hotel. The cucumber comes out as a salad beautifully dressed. The price of a cucumber changes to Rs.20/- in a small hotel to Rs.200/- in a five-star hotel where it is served on a silver platter.

These insights on the transition and moving up the value chain amazed all the other cucumbers.

If a simple cucumber can increase its price, why can't you with your vast resources?

Review the pricing of your products and services. Are you stuck at a price band that existed a long time ago? Have you not had the guts to raise the pricing just because you are scared of the competition? Underselling is not the way to expand markets. Cheap products often make their customers doubt their quality.

Many of you may want to refrain from hiking the prices of your products and services. Whenever it is time to hike the prices, the mind feels a little insecure and wonders whether this hike will result in a dip in the sales. You are scared of all the things that can happen because of the hiked prices. You fear losing your customers to the competition. And you are stranded forever with the pricing that you started with. You complain about increasing costs and inflation but do not pass on these costs on to the price. More than market dependent the pricing is mind dependent. In your mind if you sell yourself cheap then it is your problem.

One has to keep moving up the value chain. I implore you to back it with a bold decision and hike your price. What you must do is to be true to yourself and justify this new price. Whenever you hike the price genuinely, your customers will respect it and will expect you to deliver value for their money. They will not mind the price hike provided you keep up the quality of your product or service.

Increase your comfort zone. Test market this new upward pricing and you will realize Voila! Things just fall in place.

The Snowball Effect

*There is only one boss. The customer.
And he can fire everybody in the
company from the chairman on down,
simply by spending his money
somewhere else.*

— Sam Walton

An avalanche begins with a small rock or ball of snow that rolls down a slope. It gains momentum and starts increasing in size, gathering more snow on the way. And then, more and more snow starts sliding down. Avalanches are quite catastrophic as they rush down thousands of tons of snow, burying people, animals, houses and debris of entire villages.

Avalanches are some of the worst natural disasters that claim both life and property.

The same principle works for money too. As growth happens in a succession of events, downfall is also a chain of events and not a particular event in isolation.

Attack the problem at the start and nip it in the bud to avoid setbacks later on. And the vicious chain of bad events breaks.

To create a series of growth events, don't restrict the flow. Don't even pause to count your money lest you become complacent or divert your mind from your goal to reaching financial growth. If you take a slightly longer pause, you might begin to doubt your own growth potential. So, just keep moving. This is known as 'riding the wave'.

You will see this reflecting in your daily life. Sometimes, your day starts with something really nice. Co-incidentally, the entire day is full of happy incidents and is quite pleasant. The momentum created in the beginning of the chain triggered all the latter incidents to fall into their right place.

This process will always operate — consciously or un-consciously. Don't wait for an avalanche to happen, you create one.

There Are Many
Idiots at the Top

You reach a point where you don't work for money.

— *Walt Disney*

Like they say there is plenty of space at the top, but what if this space is occupied by too many dumb and incompetent idiots?

By our definition, idiots are incompetent people who may be a part of your organization. Either they're lucky to be in the right place at the right time or are there by virtue of playing office politics or buttering the top bosses. Every organization nurtures a group of good-for-nothings who are good only at pleasing their seniors. Sadly, such people only hamper the organization's growth and the spirit of its employees. Moreover, such people are highly competent in the art of pleasing the top management by hook or crook, despite being completely useless and unproductive.

As you read this, you might either feel happy that someone is actually addressing this issue or you might get a little agitated. If your reaction is the former one, there is no problem. But if you're getting a little angry, I'm worried. You are probably showing certain 'idiot' characteristics. Well, if you have realized this, do make positive changes in yourself.

In the perspective of an organization, idiots have a peculiar quality. Once they manage to reach the top, then they like to form a herd of similar idiots. They are very comfortable with their breed around them especially since they feel highly threatened amidst the wise and competent. They do everything to ensure that the competent people are kept busy in their own activities. They are called the 'Money Drainers'. Such people drain opportunity and precious resources in organi-zations.

Idiots exist because they succeed in pampering the egos of the top management and playing politics in their organizations. You have to now choose whether you would want to choose to be the 'idiot' who will reach nowhere or the competent person who would surely become more productive and wealthy. Show the idiots the door.

Do an idiot cleaning session or just watch yourself being clean bowled.

The One-Man Army

Disneyland is a work of love. We didn't go into Disneyland just with the idea of making money.

— Walt Disney

Somewhere in your organization is one person who can be termed as a 'One-Man Army'. This person may or may not be known to you but is directly or indirectly responsible for your success.

Sometimes a single person can be as effective as a team of 50 people and any number of machines. The human factor can never be replaced by any amount of technology. Sadly, many large organizations do not realize this and therefore do not value their human resources. They therefore do not allocate proper resources to develop their employees and ensure employee satisfaction. All the same, there are many others who do the exact opposite and thus create happy employees and happier customers.

World history is replete with examples of metamorphoses of

tiny organizations into huge multinationals. There are examples also of organizations being totally wiped out with the entry of wrong characters and exit of the right ones.

Look for that Magical Face in your organization. It could be hidden behind the faces that you see around you. Give recognition to that face. Respect, be grateful and show your gratitude to the person who has that face. When you invest in Human Potential, your cash registers will keep ringing joyously.

It is Time to Buy a Big Fat Lock

Advertising is the art of convincing people to spend money they don't have for something they don't need.

— Will Rogers

Whatever field you are in, the key essence to growth is commitment to the business itself. Along with commitment, comes an eye for detail, an ability to aim for perfection and progress. In the ultimate bargain, nothing works better than this.

An unattended customer is standing for a long time waiting for your attention; your product is unavailable, you have incompetent people working for you, uncourteous salespeople. This may sound like a recipe for disaster. If you don't raise your standards of professional service — if you're too slow to catch up with the pace of change — with a disorganized set-up and a lack of personal interest to run the show and many more such issues, then be sure to see the bottom of the ocean because your ship is sinking faster than the Titanic.

An incident in the life of a careless shopkeeper

Customer: (to the shopkeeper): "Could anyone attend me please?"

Shopkeeper: (sleepily): "Yes, tell me what do you want?"

Customer: "Is this product available?"

Shopkeeper: (searching slowly and after a long time) "NO"

Customer: "What about other brands like…." (names some brands)

Shopkeeper: (half eyes closed) "Out of stock."

Customer: "Can you take an order so you can reach it to me later?"

Shopkeeper: "In our management practice, we don't accept orders in advance."

Irritated Customer: "Can I talk to the owner?"

Shopkeeper: "He is not here at the moment."

Customer: (highly irritated) "Do you have a big fat lock?"

Shopkeeper: "No, why?"

Customer: "Buy it fast because you are going to need it soon."

Money flow demands doing certain things in an effective manner. A business should be looked after with commitment and dedication otherwise it will not be long before you will need a big fat lock adorning your office or business premise, forever.

Money and Your Magical Touch

Money and women are the most sought after and the least known about of any two things we have.

— Will Rogers

Each and every money transaction has a person behind it. The more you acknowledge his or her face and build a rapport, the more enriched will be your experience. The days of the merciless boss are gone. Today, employers are looking at building a more open employer-employee relationship. In fact, the 'open door' policy that started in the West has also caught attention in India. Employees can freely approach their employers or bosses and freely discuss practically everything.

Personal contact with employees has great benefits. It motivates them and gives them a sense of belonging. It also gives you an in-depth understanding as to how things are progressing in the organization. It is all about pausing a while each day to tell your workers how much you value them. Do appreciate their contribution to your company's growth. You could put a little heart and soul into this activity and ask them genuinely about personal fulfillment and family well-being before handing over the cheque for the month.

The money element, also has something more to it. It has your genuine concern for your worker's welfare attached. This money goes further than just satisfying the monetary needs of your employee. It touches his heart, mind and soul and that of his family too.

It is well-known that a doctor cures a patient more with his kind words and warmth than by the pills he prescribes. A good doctor builds confidence and hope in his patient rather than making him feel dejected and worried. He says, "This pill will make you healthy, cheerful and fit even before you know it." These magical words work wonders and help the patient to make a speedy recovery. And a patient who has been cured in this way may well become a friend for life.

It is a good idea to have kind and courteous words for persons you meet. For example, you have bought something at a departmental store. While paying a simple "Thanks for your courteous service" and a few additional comments like "Your shop is very aesthetically done or "It is a pleasure shopping at your place" will go a long way for generating a healthy relationship. You look forward to shopping in that place. You will always be welcomed in such a place.

Develop the magical touch everywhere you go. Before you hand over money, always think how you can make the money go a longer distance from the hand to the heart.

When Being Small Is Actually Great

A successful man is one who makes more money than his wife can spend. A successful woman is one who can find such a man.

— Lana Turner

GrowBig.com had a small beginning with only a handful of employees. Soon, things just fell into place. The Dot Com fever started and Grow Big grew into a really big organization. Its employees increased in number, its turnover doubled, its location spread and grew, all within a time of one year. It attracted the best of professionals. Employees earned well and more importantly, enjoyed their job. They were highly motivated and worked with great commitment and dedication. Their offices looked like a Seven Star hotel. They could afford anything and everything.

After two years, suddenly without warning, the organization collapsed under its own weight. The reasons for this collapse were many but the one that stood out was that they could not manage the huge growth.

> Golmaal to a new would-be employer: "What kind of a company is this! In the previous company, I was given a car, a huge house and 3 servants. I often entertained my clients in Five Star hotels. I even owned the latest mobile phone.
>
> Employer: "Then why did you leave this company?"
>
> Golmaal: (Sheepishly) "Oh, the company went bust."

There are numerous examples of companies and individuals who were great while they were small. They were able to manage effectively. Lean and mean was their success mantra. But then they decided to grow and grow very fast. They could not manage their growth and eventually had to wind up. Growth itself can be a hindrance at times, if it can't be managed.

Are you one of those who cannot manage big changes or growth? If you are, be assured that you don't need to push yourself. Stop comparing yourself with others. Just be happy, content and relaxed. Stand still and allow the grass to grow beautifully.

Don't be too obsessed with the growth formula. In the process of growth if you lose more than you started with, then it has no meaning and it is best to be small.

Isn't it said, **the best things in life come in small packages.**

Conclusion

You have been brainwashed so far to be
against money. Now get brainwashed
towards money for a change.

— Suresh Padmanabhan

The Moon or the Finger

Money was never a big motivation for me, except as a way to keep score. The real excitement is playing the game.

— *Donald Trump*

A child once came running to its mother and asked, "Mamma, where is the moon?" The mother took the child out into the open and pointed to the moon with her finger. Satisfied that she had answered her child in a practical way she went off to sleep.

The next day, the child went to school. When the teacher asked, "Have you seen the moon?" the child said "Yes!" gleefully. The teacher enquired, "Can you show me the moon?" The Child pointed to his index finger and said, "This is the moon."

The child had seen its mother's finger and thought it to be the moon.

The finger is the pointer and the moon is the thing pointed to.

We too search for answers in the pointers and often lose or miss the object pointed to. Our knowledge of money is somewhat like this.

If we believe paper currency, plastic cards or coins to be money, we are missing the point. We are like the child who thinks that the finger is the moon.

So what is beyond paper currency? What is the deeper mystery of money? Where did money evolve? What is fate? What is destiny? What are the other factors that govern money? What is karma? How does karma affect us? Does astrology affect us? How does Feng Shui or Vastu impact our money flow?

There may be many such questions in your mind. I promise you all the answers in my 'Money Workshop'. Do attend the Money Workshop if you don't want to live in ignorance and wish to dissolve/resolve all your questions about money. An unanswered question in your mind may be blocking money flow into your life. Seek your answers and clear your way to wealth and abundance of money and success. The solutions to your problems are now not beyond your reach.

The Money Workshop — All about Money and Beyond It.

Experience it Live

Don't marry for money. You can borrow it cheaper.

— Scottish proverb

Where materialism and spirituality go hand in hand.

A journey is said to be complete only when you experience it fully and enjoy it. Even if I describe a dessert in minute details, it is of no use unless you get to taste the real dish. If I were to describe the scenic beauty of the Himalayas, what use is it unless you experience the view yourself, isn't it? It's almost like expecting light and warmth from a painting of the Sun.

Therefore, in the Indian tradition a lot of importance was given to the 'real experience'. Words cannot go beyond a certain extent to describe the deeper truths. A live physical presence is a must.

This is why I advise you to attend the Money Workshop, live. Money Workshop is a two days intense program on money, wealth creation, abundance and prosperity. When you dive into this ocean and delve deep, the experience too becomes deeper and crystallizes. If you want quick breakthroughs, perfect solutions, enhanced powers, and want to see yourself on the path of prosperity, you must attend the Money Workshop.

There is a session titled 'The Ultimate Truth' which could be the most potent session that you might ever attend. This unravels the ultimate truth of money, your own Personal Power, and the deepest of the Spiritual Powers and about the God/Universe. This session is so powerful that after attending this session everything in life just falls into place. As part of the workshop, you will learn amazing mental techniques and powers. These techniques when used will help you solve almost any problem you face in life. You can then lead the most powerful life with, essences you gather in the Ultimate Truth session.

It is said, 'When the disciple is ready, the Master appears.' Similarly, when you are ready for the deeper truths, the Money Workshop will appear.

One Book One Hope

A bank is a place where they lend you an umbrella in fair weather and ask for it back when it rains.

— Robert Frost

A new beginning, a new job, a promotion, a new customer, a breakthrough, a lottery, a new picture, a new idea, a dream fulfilled, a fat cheque, a project, a burning desire, an assignment, a discovery, an invention, a good screenplay, a direction, a song, a good stock pick, a well-timed investment, a stroke of good luck, a good life partner, a worthy friend, another opportunity, one more life, one more hit, one more success, one right call, one breath, one right step, one miracle, one magic, one smile, one deal, one more day, one look, one more heart-beat, one meeting, one journey, one yes, one win, one call, one right network, one world, one new meaning, one more chance, just one...

Any change requires just one moment. Never give up on hope. Welcome the next moment for it will be yours... just for a moment!

It is your birthright to be rich, happy and prosperous. Claim it and enjoy the most wonderful life from today onwards...

A Gift for Someone Who I Value, Love and Respect

For thousands of years, books have been the best of friends to the loneliest of hearts. Books have helped people grow in knowledge, wisdom, and self-power. Books have transformed people from their state of sadness to happiness, from darkness of despair to light of hope, and spread smiles around. Books have actually transported young and old into a world of fantasy, where anything and everything is lovely, beautiful and rich.

Someone close to you might just need a helping hand in his or her life with regard to money. Gift them this book, *I Love Money*. It may prove to be a new lease of life for someone you love. We all love to gift something thoughtful, meaningful and everlasting to our dear ones to remember us by. Your friends will remember you and bless you with all their heart when they flourish in their lives and reap the benefits of *I Love Money*. Yes, whenever something beautiful happens in their money world, you will surely receive their blessings.

Corporate houses and organizations could also gift their employees or customers *I Love Money*. This would definitely add value to their life helping them realize all their dreams and ambitions.

Money Consciousness

It isn't necessary to be rich and famous to be happy. it's only necessary to be rich.

— Alan Alda

Once in the kingdom of Janak, there lived two poets — Ram and Shyam. Both poets were equally gifted. Ram believed that his poetic talent would always keep him prosperous and he always felt grateful to God for his talent. On the other hand, Shyam always worked a little harder at appeasing the King to make his gold mohars. He concentrated more on getting the King's favours.

The King wondered why Ram was always prosperous while Shyam, despite his extra effort, did not earn much. He called his minister and told him to find out why this happened.

The minister invited both the poets to the court the following day very early in the morning. Meanwhile, with the help of the other courtiers he devised a plan to test them. He was aware that both would cross the bridge before they reached the palace gates, and planned to keep a bag of diamonds on the bridge just to entice them.

Early next morning, Shyam reached the bridge first; the courtiers and the minister were happy that Shyam would see the bag of diamonds and take it. They kept a close watch on him from a distance. Shyam did not notice the bag and crossed the bridge and Ram who was just behind him picked it up and thanked Existence/God for it.

The King, who was standing at the end of the bridge, stopped Shyam and asked him why he had not picked up the bag. Shyam was too confused. He told the King, that he had not seen any bag. Since the bridge was deserted that day, he had walked across it with his eyes closed. He later told the King that he always had the desire to cross the bridge with his eyes closed. Ram who was more tuned to prosperity noticed the bag while crossing the bridge and got it.

The King then decided to ensure that the gift reached Shyam. And so after their poetry session, he gifted Shyam with a water melon filled with precious stones and Ram with apples. Next day he asked the minister to call them to the court. When they arrived he asked Shyam if a miracle had occurred yesterday. Shyam said nothing unusual had happened. When the King asked Shyam, "What did you do with the water melon yesterday?" Shyam said that since the water melon was heavy he had exchanged it for the apples with Ram.

Ram thanked the Almjghty and told the King that he had received precious stones in the water melon as a gift.

The minister later informed the King that this always happened to Ram because he was more tuned to prosperity than Shyam was.

Similarly, after reading *I Love Money*, you too will subconsciously sow the seeds of money consciousness. Consistently working on your thoughts and taking appropriate actions you will become more finely tuned. Then watch how the whole Universe schemes things magically for you that will bring you Money, Prosperity and Happiness at your door step.

When you are tuned to Money Consciousness, Money comes to you in leaps and bounds.

Your Own Success Story

When a person with money meets a person with experience, the person with the experience winds up with the money and the person with the money winds up with the experience.

— Harvey MacKay

We would be glad to hear from you. Do keep writing in, your success stories: *info@themoneyworkshop.com* and *www.themoneyworkshop.com*. Someone somewhere might just need a reminder that the techniques work.

As you share your experiences and life's varied colours with others, you will touch many lives. You will also be able to interpret life better and use these techniques in a more effective manner.

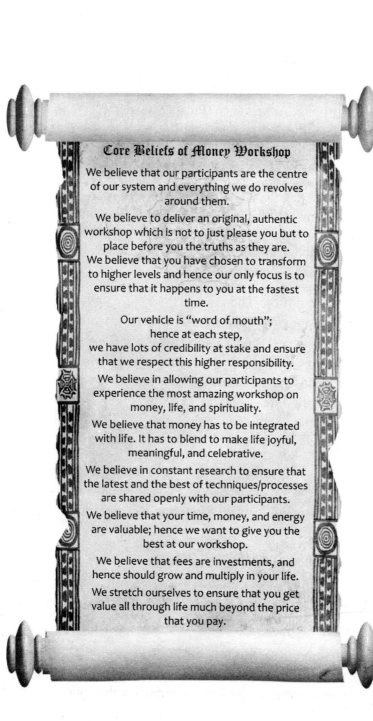

Core Beliefs of Money Workshop

We believe that our participants are the centre of our system and everything we do revolves around them.

We believe to deliver an original, authentic workshop which is not to just please you but to place before you the truths as they are.
We believe that you have chosen to transform to higher levels and hence our only focus is to ensure that it happens to you at the fastest time.

Our vehicle is "word of mouth";
hence at each step,
we have lots of credibility at stake and ensure that we respect this higher responsibility.

We believe in allowing our participants to experience the most amazing workshop on money, life, and spirituality.

We believe that money has to be integrated with life. It has to blend to make life joyful, meaningful, and celebrative.

We believe in constant research to ensure that the latest and the best of techniques/processes are shared openly with our participants.

We believe that your time, money, and energy are valuable; hence we want to give you the best at our workshop.

We believe that fees are investments, and hence should grow and multiply in your life.

We stretch ourselves to ensure that you get value all through life much beyond the price that you pay.

Divine Prosperity Shop

You could choose to order amazing and useful products from our Divine Prosperity Shop

1. *I Love Money* — English, Tamil, Hindi, Marathi, Telugu, Gujarati, Kannada etc.

2. Money Mantras (Vol 1-2) – Audio CD
Powerful Mantras to recover your stuck money, attract material prosperity, remove blocks pertaining to money, mantras to enhance planetary influence and other mystical mantras for wealth creation – Volume 1-2.

3. New Age Music Therapy
Awesome musical composition to uproot emotional pain and negativity. Powerful music that will flood your life with joy and bliss. Powerful mantras which will make your day brighter filled with posite energy and joy.
Good Morning Life – Audio CD
Sunshine Life – Audio CD
Happy Mind – Audio CD

4. Conscious Spending and Savings – DVD
Tips by Suresh Padmanabhan in English on how to save more money – (Bonus Video on Money and manifesting Desires in Life).

5. Powerful Spiritual Secrets of Money – DVD
Tips by Suresh Padmanabhan in English on connection between Spirituality and Money – (Bonus Video on receiving and giving Money).

6. I Love Money – Incense Sticks
Designer incense sticks made with natural herbs (mentioned in ancient sacred manuscripts) and saturated with exotic perfumes.

This incense is reported to draw good things — luck, money, love and success. It can be used in homes and offices to cleanse the premise of any negative or unwanted energies, restore, maintain peace and serenity in the home and work-place

(9) Sankalpa Siddhi – Incense Sticks
This incense stick will facilitate that amazing relaxed state of mind as mentioned in Indian shastras, where your mind becomes a fertile soil to sow the seeds of your desires. This can be used for meditations and relaxation.

To purchase any of above products, Contact

Sawanna Enterprises
No. 57, 1st Floor, Puttanna Road,
Basavanagudi, Bangalore-560 004
P: +91 80 2660 7011
M : (0) 90363 12786
E: info@sawannabooks.com

About the Author

Suresh Padmanabhan is an author, a public speaker, a columnist, and the creator of Money Workshop. He has also conducted some amazing workshops like 'Sankalpa Siddhi', 'Ancient Secrets of Complete Well-being', and 'Veda of Life'. His book *I Love Money* has been translated into 11 Indian and foreign languages and is an international best seller. He has toured widely all over the world conducting Money Workshops for the last 12 years.

His talks have been telecast worldwide through Zee networks, a leading TV channel. He has spoken to more than a million people worldwide and corporates on topics connected with self-growth, money, wealth creation, spirituality, and stock markets. He is a columnist with leading magazines.

His forthcoming books *On cloud 9* (the first in the series of trilogy on women), *Only, Profits* (on how to create wealth through investing and the stock market), and other books on subjects useful to one and all. All his workshops and books are in-depth, full of intensity and can be applied on a day-to-day basis.

He loves the wisdom of Ancient India—the rich lineage of Rishi's, Guru's, and Masters; feels the completeness in their teachings; and believes that India has timeless wisdom to share with the world.

All his works will reflect this philosophy.

He loves travelling, connecting with wonderful people, and writing. He is proud to be an Indian and wants the world to recognize the rich heritage of India. His aim is to impact millions of people worldwide and raise their level of consciousness in all areas, especially pertaining to Money, Life, and Spirituality.

Our Other Popular Workshops

Practical Insights to Catapult You into Huge Success Materialistically and Spiritually

Sankalpa Siddhi

- Secrets of Manifestation, laws of attraction and other higher universal laws
- The power to create what you want now in your mind and hands......
- The western movie Secret created a lot of interest in the world of Manifestation.
- Now add more power and techniques of the East to make your journey complete...

Ancient Secrets of Complete Well-being
(Basic to Advanced Levels)

Dive into Ancient India's Unrevealed Hidden Secrets of Mind, Body and Soul.

- Identify the best process for Inner Mastery for Women and Men
- Unheard secrets of Prana
- Instant control of Mind, using the Power of Nadi
- Cut off from Negative Thoughts and focus on What you want
- Field Aura Cleansing
- 20 finger Earthing and more instant secrets
- Zap off your excess weight effortlessly
- Esoteric principles of the Body and Mind
- Right and Wrong Foods and their impact on Annamaya Kosha

- Ancient Indian Secrets to be Disease Free for a Life Time
- Experience the forgotten language of talking with your body
- Learn to switch on and switch off your mind at will

Attend with your family for an Unforgettable Experience of a life time.

For Powerful Insights on Money, Life & Spirituality follow us on

www.themoneyworkshop.com

www.themoneyworkshop.com/blog

facebook.com/moneyworkshop

twitter.com/moneyworkshop

in.linkedin.com/in/moneyworkshop

youtube.com/themoneyworkshop

For Schedules & other details Contact our associates

Chennai	Ravi Padmanabhan :	+91 98414 38486
Bangalore	Jameel :	+91 98452 24979
Delhi	Sandeep Goswamy :	+91 98181 81991
Mumbai	Yogesh Naik :	+91 98205 91354
Pune	Shriram Modak :	+91 98224 09016
	Gauri Ambekar:	+91 94235 70135
Gujarat	Nimish Mehta :	+91 98251 38415

Write to us at *info@themoneyworkshop.com*

Thanking you from the bottom of our heart.